THOMAS G. KANDIAH

THE HARDSHIP OF GROWING UP ON WHEELS

A Memoir

authorHOUSE

AuthorHouse™ UK
1663 Liberty Drive
Bloomington, IN 47403 USA
www.authorhouse.co.uk
Phone: 0800.197.4150

Published by AuthorHouse 11/12/2018

ISBN: 978-1-7283-8059-9 (sc)
ISBN: 978-1-7283-8058-2 (e)

I dedicate this to Kim and Rachel
For helping me go through this journey.

CONTENTS

NOTE TO THE READER

Just a quick note before we begin:

Everything is written from my point of view.

I am writing this five years or more after the events, so please forgive me if I get some dates or moments in the wrong order.

Lastly, due to the sensitivity of topics I talk about, I have changed the majority of people's names.

OK, with that out of the way, let's begin.

Where It All Began

Hello, everyone. My name is Thomas George Kandiah. I was born on 26 January 1994 at King George Hospital. I was taken straight to the special care baby unit (SCBU) because there were some complications I don't know much about.

I had a normal childhood despite living with a disability and endless trips to the hospital. I had no idea what was going on. In my early years, all I can remember is playing the recorder in nursery and singing songs in primary.

I keep hearing from people of all ages that high school covers the best years of your life, and those memories will be with you forever. Most of your best friends then will be with you for a very long time. However, this has not been the case for me. In my short twenty-four years of living on this planet, I can say that high school has been the worst six years yet—with a tiny drop of the best days of my life. In fact, this must be the hardest part to write, because I have to try to remember those moments and tell you what happened to me in my school years.

2

School Induction Day 2004

It all started when my parents and I looked at school induction days. There were only two local to where we lived at the time: Valentines High School and Seven Kings High School. Valentines High School was my neighbour school. So we went to see what the school was like and its general feel. When we got to the school, we were taken into a science taster class, where the teacher told us about the school.

This was the first time in my life when I experienced an uneasiness on high stools. I was helped up onto the seat, and the moment my bottom landed on it, I felt very anxious. I leaned over the desk and grabbed the edge of the table. My helper saw that I was uncomfortable on the stool and asked the teacher if I could use the teacher's chair. I was so much better with the other chair, I couldn't believe it. On that day I realised that I wasn't happy with anything with too much height.

After visiting the school, our group had lunch in Valentines Park, right next to the school. I thought it was cool having a park as a school playground. But knowing my luck, I reckoned there were probably rules governing the park.

After lunch, we went back to school to finish the day.

#

For me, leaving primary school was hard because I had a good group of friends. I remember walking onto the playground, heading towards a cab to take me home. I looked around, and everyone was crying their eyes out because they were going to different schools and thought they would never see each other again. Seeing my friends all sad and crying choked me up a bit. I waited till I got into the cab, looked back at the school, and took a photo. Then I felt something on my cheek. I rubbed it off. When the cab driver asked if I was OK, I just said yes, and we drove home.

#

A few weeks later, I had a date set to go to Seven Kings High School. My parents chose this school because Seven Kings had the best facilities for people with disabilities. My dad dropped me off at the gates and said, "Good luck, Tom." I headed to the front entrance of the school. At this time, I used an electric wheelchair, so moving myself past the speed bumps was easy and took me no effort.

When I got through to the entrance, they directed me to the main hall and told me where to park myself. All wheelchair users were being told to be at the back of the hall. I was a bit early and was the only wheelchair user there. I looked around at the hall and saw hundreds of empty seats. I couldn't believe how many seats there were. Slowly, more people entered the hall and sat down.

I had picked up my induction pack, but I didn't pay any attention to it as I was so nervous. Then, from the corner of my eye, I saw a pair of small wheels from another wheelchair. I thought, *Yes, finally, another person in a wheelchair. I'm not the only one.*

As I looked up, a teacher parked the other wheelchair next to mine and said, "Tom, this is Sarah. Sarah, this is Tom."

Then I looked into Sarah's dark-brown eyes. We both reached over to shake each other's hands at the same time. She said, "Hello," and smiled.

I got butterflies in my stomach as soon as she spoke. After a very short pause, I smiled back and said, "Hello." At that moment I knew my future was going to be bright in this school.

After everyone entered, the head of school, Sir Alan Steer, stood and gave us a warm welcome to Seven Kings High School.

3

Year Seven: 2005–2006

A few months later, the first day of school came. I wore my new uniform and carried a school bag. When the school bus arrived, they helped me on and then strapped me in. I was very nervous. The bus picked up more students along the way, and we headed off to our new school for the first time.

When I got to school, I went into my new classroom for the coming year. I asked the teacher where I should sit, and she parked me at the desk nearest the door.

The learning support assistant (LSA) in high school was much different from primary school. I now had a new helper for each lesson. It was scary for me to try and develop some sort of friendship with each of them.

As the year went on, I struggled to make friends. I had trouble blending into the crowd and getting noticed. Every lunchtime, the other students went to the fields and played football or cricket. I was on the sidelines, watching them. I thought about ways to get people to at least notice me.

I think by this time, England had won the 2005 Ashes, so I had the cricket hype. I brought my cricket bat and a tennis ball to school and stored them in my locker; they only just fit. As soon as my classmates saw the cricket bat, they asked me if they could check it out and if I would give them a game at lunchtime.

When the fourth lesson ended, I looked out the window to check if the weather cleared. I was pleased to see the sky was a perfect blue, without a cloud in sight. I powered my way through the herd of people trying to get to the fields, found a vacant spot at the corner of the field, and waited. To my surprise, students came. I couldn't believe it. I batted and bowled, and I refused to step down. I managed to play for something like forty-five minutes, almost collapsing from lack of water.

As lunchtime ran out, I knew I had to get a drink. I rushed to the cafeteria. There were table tennis tables in the way, and I was so busy talking about the Ashes, I wasn't paying any attraction to where I was going. Bang! A rush of pain started in my fingers and travelled up my arm. Without realising it, I had smashed into a table with my left armrest, driving it under the table and snapping the joystick off. By the time I discovered what I'd done, the person with me was saying, "Wait here while I go to the medical centre to get help." My chair couldn't move, so no worries on that part.

Now, the cafeteria and the medical centre were at opposite ends of the school. I sat there for ten minutes and began to panic as lessons were starting. An LSA came over to help move my chair from underneath the table. We collected the pieces of my chair that had fallen off. Then the LSA pushed me to the medical centre to check out my left hand and to see if the staff could repair my chair. They taped my ring and middle fingers together and managed to fix most of my chair.

Meanwhile, someone left my cricket bat and tennis ball in my locker. In the days that followed my accident, people asked to use my cricket bat. At first I was OK with it. When I was better, with my fingers fixed, I joined them during some lunchtimes. But I noticed that gradually, I was getting less and less playing time. I realised I was being pushed out of the group, and I lost interest in cricket altogether. I took the bat home, where I knew it would be safe. Students still asked me for the bat, but I told them I had taken it home. They were disappointed, but what could I say? It was my bat. If I couldn't use it, what was the point?

When My Life Changed for the Better

Very early in the year—I think it was still the first month of starting school—I was in a science taster lesson. The teacher gave us many games and split us into groups of four or five. This was how the school tried to make us talk to everyone and build friendships. Sadly, I can't remember what we were doing in the lessons. Maybe something to do with water jet rocket bottles.

The teacher gave instructions on what to do. I sat in my wheelchair amid the stools, trying to hear the group talk. The science tables were really tall, and I felt small in my wheelchair. All of a sudden, a girl in my group turned and got my attention. She asked if I knew the girl who was also in a wheelchair, Sarah.

I responded with a nervous, "Yes." I'm not sure why, but the height difference made me feel intimidated.

"Do you like Sarah?"

I nodded.

"Aw, do you *like* like her?"

For a split second, I didn't know what that meant. Then I felt a knot in my gut. My face burned up around the cheeks as I put it together.

"Oh my God!" the girl exclaimed. "You're blushing! That's cute." Then she started singing! "*Tom and Sarah sitting in a tree, K-I-S-S-I-N-G!*"

She stopped singing and said, "Do you know that a little birdie whispered to me that Sarah *like* likes you?"

I couldn't believe it.

For the rest of the lessons, I was distracted. I thought, *Hang on, I do indeed have feelings towards Sarah*. Before that day I hadn't thought of our friendship that way. She had simply been the only person I could talk to without being nervous, and she fully understood every word I said. Don't get me wrong: it was only small talk at the time, but it really meant a lot to me. No other student would listen or could quite understand what I was trying to say.

It was difficult for most people who didn't know me well to understand me because, at that age, I had a stammer. The stammer made it hard to understand the words that I was trying to say. That in turn made it difficult for me to make friends. I went to the speech therapist to help me with the sound of the letter *L*, as an example. My disability affected my tongue movement, which made any word with the letter *L* difficult to say correctly. Over the years, this has improved. However, it does get worse if I feel nervous, scared, or uneasy.

On the day my classmate told me about Sarah's feelings, my life changed forever. I couldn't concentrate on most lessons; my mind was elsewhere. I didn't want to ask Sarah straight away if this rumour was true. If it were false, I would look like the biggest fool in school. So I lay low and waited for the opportunity to bring it up without scaring her.

Days turned into weeks, and weeks turned into months. It was harder to hide my true feelings as talking to her became easier and more comfortable. After about three months, though, an opportunity came up in a design and technology class. We were told to make a keyring out of acrylic. The teacher said we should note down any ideas, then draw up a sketch outline of our favourite design.

So there I was, staring at my A3-size paper for ten minutes, and still no ideas came. Mrs Hamlett, my helper for that lesson, walked by and saw that I had nothing on my sheet. She sat down and tried to come up with some suggestions. After the third idea or so, she said, "How about a heart? You know, for you-know-who."

I was slightly embarrassed because this was the second person who had inferred some sort of idea how I felt for Sarah. I whispered, "Yes, sure. Can you help me draw one?"

Then the teacher reminded us that we had to use two assorted colours and mould them together. On the day of choosing the colours, I was slightly disappointed that after the colour red, the only other colour available was black.

I was using the heavy equipment to cut one of the hearts out, and the other students noticed my design. They teased me, saying things like, "Who you are going to give this to, Tom?" The helper told me to take no notice, and that I was doing a wonderful thing.

After a few weeks of working with my helper, the idea on the sheet of paper had become a tangible thing in the palm of my hand. Here is what the end product looked like:

After I made the key ring, I was picked up by Max, my childminder, to go to his house. I refused to take off my blazer. It was in the middle of a heatwave, and I kept it on for the whole time that I was at his house.

A few days later, on the hottest day of the summer, Max's wife, Irene, persuaded me to take my blazer off. I took it off with help from Max. It was a bit of a struggle, and the key ring fell out of a pocket, hitting the floor. I didn't realise it until I had sat back down on the chair.

Max picked it up. "What's this?"

I went bright red in the face and said nothing.

"Who is this for—anyone special?" he persisted.

"No one," I replied quickly, hoping both of them would move on and forget the subject. Max put the key ring back into the jacket pocket.

The very next day at his house, I was sitting in a swinging chair. Soon after I had settled down, the doorbell rang. Max's family had come over to visit; our families had been friends for years. After everyone had said hello and settled down, either in the kitchen or the front room, I overheard Max saying, "Jo, did you know Tom's got a lady friend?"

Jo replied "No!"

Everyone became interested.

Jo said, "What's her name, Tom?"

Again, I went as red as a cherry.

Many voices joined in. "What's going on? Tom's got a crush on someone!" Suddenly, they started singing! *"Tom and Sarah sitting in a tree, K-I-S-S-I-N-G!"*

Seeing me all shy, Max said, "Cheer up, Tom! We're only messing with you."

Moving on a few weeks, it continued to get harder to keep my feelings to myself. I had begun to think that everyone knew I had feelings for someone. I sat in my room and thought, *It's time to gamble with fate and see if Sarah feels the same way.*

So, one lunchtime, I finished my meal and went over to the medical centre. Most of us hung out there. I checked the first room on the left.

Someone said, "Hi, Tom, come in and—"

"Not now, kinda busy," I said, scanning the room. *She's not in this one*, I thought, and moved on to the next room, two doors down on the right.

Sarah was in there, chatting away to people. I knew her pain wasn't bothering her that day, because she was moving about easily without her wheelchair. I sat half in and half out of the doorway, with my hands on either side of the frame.

"You all right, Tom? You looked distracted," someone in the room said.

"Oh, y-yes, I'm fine."

I sat in the doorway for ten minutes or so, the butterflies building to the point where I had to excuse myself. I headed outside to get some fresh air, all the time saying to myself, "Come on, you can do this." A minute passed, and I thought, *I'm just going to ask her and see what happens.*

I moved back to the room, checking my inside pocket for the key ring. "Sarah, could I speak to you for a minute?" I said, trying to sound confident.

"Yes, sure," she replied.

I had the key ring now clutched in my right hand. A million thoughts buzzed through my brain. I turned around and saw her beautiful eyes. "Sarah ..."

Someone walked in just as I was going to speak.

I thought, *Come on! No more distractions.* I waited for the person to walk by. I very quickly composed myself, and only just managed to say, "Do you ..." Then, for some reason, I stopped.

With confusion on her face, Sarah prompted, "Do I ...?"

The universe seemed stuck in time. Everything froze.

I tried again. "Sarah … do … you …" I realised I still had the key ring, so I opened my hand to show her.

She knew exactly what I was trying to say. Her body language tightened up and her cheeks turned every shade of red. With a slight smile, she gave a tiny nod. "Do you like me?" she whispered.

I almost missed what she said. My heart was racing faster and faster. *Come on, just say it!* my head was screaming at me. "Y-y-y-yes."

As soon as I said that, she went back into the room, grabbed her school bag, and walked off to her next lesson. I was confused. I heard students whispering, "Did Tom just ask Sarah out?"

For the next few days, all I kept hearing was people talking about me asking Sarah out. At the end of one school day, I was getting geared up on the bus. I looked over to my left, and I saw Sarah getting on her bus. She sat down, looked over, and saw me. I blew her a kiss, and she smiled. Then I saw two other boys on the same bus, messing around and blowing kisses back at me. They were mocking me, making fun of me. I didn't know how to respond. I looked back at Sarah. I think she was telling the boys to stop, but they didn't seem to listen. They just carried on teasing me.

By the look on her face, I could tell Sarah was very concerned for me. I tried to signal "sorry" through the glass. The boys were still mocking me. I straightened my back to look as tall as possible and automatically threw a middle finger at them, if only for a quick second. This was the first time I had ever done any sort of swearing. Before that event, I wouldn't have dreamed of swearing, didn't think it was smart in any form.

I looked back at Sarah, expecting a disappointed face. Instead, she had burst out laughing. However, I still felt bad inside for what I had done. A voice in my head said, *You shouldn't have done that.*

Sarah was still laughing. I mouthed, "I'm so sorry," and smiled for a split second. The bus helper was laughing a little too. I gazed at Sarah, shrugged, and sank a bit into my chair. My head was spinning with the same thought: *I shouldn't have done that.*

Sports Days—Youth Games 2006

About halfway through the year, the school was attending the londonyouthgames.org, like the school version of the Paralympics. Four or five schools would compete against each other, with a leader board and everything. My PE teacher came up to me and said, "Tom, I'm putting you forward as one of the members to compete for our school."

I didn't know what to expect. I had done sports events before, but this was a different school with a different group of people to work with. But I nervously agreed to do this event.

My high school was well known for its excellent facilities for children with disabilities. They had set up a sports club for disabled people. It was called the Physical Disability Club or, as most of us called it, the PD Club. It met once a week on a Monday.

The club helped us a little to train for the youth games coming up. I was told that I was put in for the bean bag throwing event, so I had some sort of idea what I was doing.

When the day came, we were told to wear our standard PE uniform, which was a polo shirt, jogging bottoms, and trainers. After the second or third lesson, we were told to go the medical centre to get checked in. After that, we headed to the coach and off we went to Mile End Leisure Centre and Stadium, where the event was held.

Halfway through the journey, an LSA or teacher came over to me and asked what I had to do in my event. It was easy to follow: get a bean bag in hand, park yourself in front of a high jump bar (the same spot each time to make it fair), and throw the bean bag over the bar to get through to next round. Keep on doing this until someone wins. It was easy enough to understand. It really didn't matter how you threw the bean bag; just get it over the bar and move on, so the next person could take a shot.

When the talk was done, I had a clear knowledge of what to do, and the LSA returned to the front of the coach. I nearly always sat at the back of the coach. It was easier that way. However, it did separate me from my friends, because they were usually in the middle somewhere.

About halfway into the trip, we were each given the Borough team T-shirt. When I'd put it on, I looked at everyone else to see what the design said. The letters were across the chest area and onto the sleeve. They read:

REDBRIDGE
BOROUGH

Before we knew it, we made it to the Leisure Centre. The coach circled around as the driver tried to find a suitable parking spot. I saw many other coaches, and a sea of people flooding into the entrance. When our group was all off the coach, I just followed the crowd and went in. I was in my electric chair, so keeping up wasn't a problem. We went through the front entrance and another set of doors to reach the outdoor field area, where we signed up and were given name tags.

It was amazing to be there, seeing people still flooding in. When I first saw what the stadium look like, I couldn't believe it. It was one of those moments when you try to take every detail in at once.

When everyone had signed up, we moved to the seating area marked for Redbridge. On the rails at the bottom, there was huge banners that read:

Balfour Beatty

LONDON Youth Games

SPORT ENGLAND

One of the LSAs came over when she saw me looking at the high jump area and said, "That's where the bean bag throwing will take place." Almost as soon I heard that, I felt butterflies deep in my stomach. I had a tad of self-doubt as this was my very first real competition. I didn't know what to expect from this day.

As the hours slowly passed by, I sat at the bottom of the Redbridge seating area, where the wheelchair users were, and watched the 100m, 200m, and 400m races play out in front of me. I rooted for Redbridge, of course. One of the races had just started when I heard someone call my name: "Tom. Tom! *Tom*! After this race, head to the high-jump area." I was excited and nervous all at once.

The Redbridge people followed the teachers while other students cheered, "Good luck, guys!" That did soften the butterflies a little bit. As we walked, I saw Sarah walking in the opposite direction. We met at the crossing, but there wasn't time to stop. I just looked at her and tried to smile to hide the butterflies. She must have picked up something from my smile, because she put her hand on my shoulder, leaned in close to my ear, and said, "Good luck, Tom." Just hearing her voice was enough to soften my nerves. Now I couldn't wait for the competition to start.

As for the competition itself, it wasn't as bad as I had been making it out to be. I made it to the final. I felt like screaming, "*Yes*, I made it to the *final three!*" while getting up and jumping on the spot.

I looked around to see if the Redbridge members were still there. There were only a few, and I was pleased to see Sarah among them. As soon as I saw her, I threw up three fingers, trying to tell her that only three people were left, and I was among the three. She held up three fingers and smiled back.

The second round went similarly to the first, with the pole a little higher now. I used the same method in my release. However, this time it fell slightly short, and the bean bag hit the bar. To my amazement, it nevertheless dropped over the other side. "*Yes*! Still in the game," I said proudly to myself. "For now."

My confidence took a massive blow on that last throw. Suddenly, I became worried. As they moved the bar higher again, more and more butterflies appeared in my stomach. I took a quick glance over my shoulder at Sarah. She met my worried eyes and gave a thumbs up, murmuring, "You can do it."

When it was my turn, I moved up to the marker and parked my chair. As soon as the bean bag touched my hands, I closed my eyes and took a deep breath. Using my fingertips, I flattened the bag. *Don't try anything different, Tom*, I thought. I opened my eyes and found the target over the bar. I raised my arm and let the bag fly. There was nothing left to do but watch.

The bag descended. I saw it in front of the bar, and my heart just stopped for a second. My throw wasn't even close. Game over! I was third place.

I slowly moved towards my Redbridge group. I got "Unlucky, Tom," from almost everyone. Now it was a waiting game until the medal handouts.

That time came at the end of the day. We were called to gather around the office area, where three people were sitting. They had records of every event that had happened during the day. They call out each one: "100m group 1, third place … in second place … and finally in first place and the winner …" They did this for every event, and there were a lot! For each person receiving a medal, the audience clapped. Near the end, my arms were burning from the repetitive motion.

At last they called out, "Bean bag throwing! In third place, Thomas Kan-deer-are!"

I was a bit confused. Someone patted me and whispered, "Tom, that's you!" Still bemused, I went up to receive my medal and to stand in the third place spot. When I got there, I forgot about them saying my name wrong and smiled as the other two got their silver and gold. When all three of us had received our medals, we faced the crowd of people. I held my medal and smiled. I looked around and saw Sarah. She was looking back at me with a big grin. As my smile got even wider, I thought, *I will get a silver or gold medal next time.*

On the journey back, everyone buzzing with excitement. Although I didn't win, I had a good day and was pleased with myself. I had learned that I was OK competing in front of a crowd of people. It didn't bother me at all, and that really surprised me. It gave me the confidence to try again next time.

4

Year Eight: 2006–2007

When the summer holidays came, I was excited to have the time to connect with Sarah and build on our bond. She came to my house to meet up with my dad, mum, and brother. At first, I was very nervous about it. You know how it is when you first invite your lady friend over to the house—you pray that the family will like her. A day or two before she came, my mum called me and my brother into the lounge and said, "Tom is having a friend over. She's a girl. That doesn't mean she's his girlfriend, just a friend who happens to be a girl."

As Mum was saying this, I tried everything I could to stop her. "Mum! You do *not* have to tell everyone!" Well, I was 12—can you blame me?

When Sarah arrived, we were all upstairs in my room, talking. I don't know what I was thinking, but I tried to wrestle with my brother Matt, grabbing his leg. I heard Sarah say in a quiet voice, "Stop it. Stop it, boys. Stop fighting!"

As soon as I heard her, I thought, *That's it. I blew it. I look like a fool in front of her. What will she think of me now?*

Sarah and I went downstairs to watch TV. Dad, who had been napping, woke up after half an hour. He came into the room with his camera and kindly told Sarah and me to sit on the couch. He made a joke or a funny noise to get us to laugh, and we did. The funny thing was that after I started laughing, I couldn't stop! Everyone laughed with me, and this went on for a while. I stopped to catch my breath—then, for no reason, I started laughing again. It was like I couldn't control myself. I was so happy to be with Sarah, I just didn't want that day to end.

When summer had ended and it was time to go back to school, I was feeling good. I was excited to see Sarah and to find out what she had done on the holidays. As the school year progressed, I became used to being comfortable in public whenever we were together.

Every day, I brought a packed lunch. At the time I had a sweet tooth for Ferrero Rocher, and I brought two sweets every day: one for me and one for Sarah. I guess I thought it was a token of what we had at the time. It's the little things that count, right?

The first thought that came into my head as I was writing this bit was of one time when we had got to the stage of playing little couple's games with each other. The sun was quite high in the sky. I was early to the lunch hall and had started eating my lunch at the "wheelchairs" table. All of a sudden, I couldn't see.

A familiar voice said, "Guess who?"

I had the biggest grin on my face as I replied, "Umm, I can't remember hearing that sound before." Of course, I was playing the game.

I heard a gasp and slight laughter. "Really! Are you sure?"

"Yes, that sound is unfamiliar to me."

Her hands moved away from my eyes and onto my shoulders, and she edged round slightly to my left side until I saw her beautiful face. "It's me, silly!"

She sat down with me, and I offered her one of my chocolates. She thought that I was going to simply hand it to her. However, I wanted to try something new. I opened the chocolate and held it gently to her mouth. I have no idea why I tried this; perhaps I was trying to be romantic. Sarah didn't complain, which pleased me.

Bullying

I can't avoid writing about this topic anymore: *bullying*. I have chills running down my spine just thinking how I'm going to write about it.

Now I must explain the jumping business, so you know what I'm talking about. I think it is a part of my disability, which is cerebral palsy.

One symptom of this is that I jump very easily. The posh term for it is *enhanced startle reflex*. Basically, any loud noise or surprise movement will cause my reflex to kick in, and my body jerks as if I am jumping out of my skin. If people are unfamiliar with seeing this, sometimes they think it is funny. Perhaps it is because many people use startling as a joke. However, it is something I can't control. As I got older, I became ashamed of this action, and thus of myself, because it made me feel so powerless and small.

In year seven, right after the whole community in the medical centre heard I had asked Sarah out, I was sitting with Sarah, listening to her talk to people in the hangout rooms. Out of nowhere, a much older boy said, "Sarah had boyfriends in her last schools, and now she's with this bum!" He pointed at me and looked at her. "I don't know what you see in him!"

I tried not to take any notice; however, it did make me feel small in front of everyone. I wanted to shake it off because I knew he was looking at me to see if I would react negatively in front of Sarah.

When he saw that I wasn't going to, he walked towards me, turned around, and farted straight in my face. Now everyone was looking at me and laughing. I kept a straight face. I had a younger brother who farted all the time; no big deal. I thought this boy had finished testing me and maybe would move on something else. But, no. A few minutes after that, he came up to me almost nose-to-nose and burped.

That was the first time when I felt I couldn't take any more. I stormed out of the medical centre, tears threatening to blast out. However, I managed to hold myself together. By the end of the day, I somehow had forgotten about what happened. I'd put on a smile, trying hard to stay positive.

My Lowest Point

In year eight, the one class that I didn't enjoy was music class. It wasn't because I didn't like music; I think music is one of the most influential types of media out there. The right tune can reach deep into a person's mind and make the body feel something that it might have forgotten. As I type this, I am listening to emotional music about love and regret, knowing it will bring me back to the moments that I'm sharing with you.

That said, learning how to write music and play an instrument didn't really interest me. This might have been due to the fact that I had one of my worst moments halfway through the year. We were learning about drums and the basics of using them safely. It became one of the moments that dominate my thoughts when I'm down.

The music teacher walked into the room and told the line of students to follow. I somehow ended up in front of the room. There were no chairs set up, just an open space in the middle. There was a large piano to the left, a couple feet from the corner, and a drum kit in the centre, almost like a theatre stage.

Since I was in front, I sat far up where I thought that students could sit. Someone said that my chair would get in the way of people behind me, so I moved to the left, near the piano. I thought, *Great, I'll get an even closer look at the drums.* A drum kit is the coolest thing in the world to a 13-year-old boy.

The moment came when the teacher sat down on his stool and started demonstrating the drums. My joy at being in front of the class changed in a matter of seconds, almost once he hit the first note. I was okay for a split second. I thought maybe this wouldn't be too much for me. Then he streamed three or four notes together. Every time he banged his foot on the pedal to sound the bass drum, I was caught by surprise. I jumped at each beat.

At first only a few people looked at me, smiles on their faces. I focused on the drums and tried to predict the movements of the teacher's foot. For some reason, this intense focus made me jump more frequently. I heard laughter. The bass thump seemed louder than the other drum sounds. My startle reflex became even more massive.

All the students were now laughing. I felt acutely embarrassed. The whole class was watching me and not the teacher. I wanted to run away—but I was trapped at the front of the classroom, with twenty-odd students between me and the exit. There was no way I could go and no LSA to help me.

The only option I had was to hide. Luckily, I was parked near a giant piano. I started my chair and moved behind it, trying to shield myself from the sight of the class.

I was still jumping at the bass drum sound. Every so often, I opened one eye to look at the clock, thinking, *Hurry up! Go faster, time!* Of course, watching the time seems to make it go slower. Or am I the only one who thinks that way?

After half an hour, the bell went off. I got out as quickly as possible. I might have accidentally run over a few ankles, but I was so focused on getting away that I didn't realise. It was as if my entire world had turned into a dark tunnel, and all I could see was a tiny dot that was the exit, moving away as fast as I could wheel towards it. The dinner ladies in the corridor told me to slow down, but I didn't pay any attention to them. I knew my top speed was no faster than a person walking at a quick pace.

For the rest of that day, I felt so lonely, as if a dark cloud had formed above my head. I sat at home, eating dinner or watching TV, and slowly my mind tried to put away my feelings of disappointment and place a smile on my face. Yet the memory became more painful the longer I kept it to myself. However, if you ignore a problem and your feelings about it, it will gradually consume your thoughts. That time soon arrived.

I got the sense that the dark cloud was getting larger, consuming me in a shadow. A few days after the event, I was lying on my bed after school, and all of a sudden I couldn't take it anymore. Dad came in and asked me if I was all right. The conversation started off calmly; then I just unleashed all my thoughts and anger that had been building up in my mind. I couldn't contain myself. I screamed at the top of my lungs, "I can't take it anymore! *Don't make me go into school*! I DON'T WANNA LIVE ANYMORE!"

That's all I can remember of the conversation. It was the first time in my life when I completely lost it. I didn't think about what was coming out of my mouth, and for that moment, I didn't care. Pure anger made me say those words. I guess it was good to get the feelings out in the open instead of letting them eat me alive from the inside.

My father said, "You don't really mean what you are saying. Everybody has ups and downs. You are still going to attend school as normal."

After the eruption, I was quiet for the rest of the day. I stayed in bed, looking up at the ceiling, trying to organise my thoughts. I slowly drifted off to sleep.

The next day, I didn't want to go to school. I tried to sleep in and miss my bus to school. It didn't work. The bus turned up, and Mum came charging into my room. She woke me up, got me dressed, and hustled me onto the bus. It took all of about five minutes. Everybody on the bus then asked me if I was all right. "Rough night, Tom?"

"You can say that," I replied sleepily and shrugged. They thought I was just tired from waking up minutes ago. I was like that until I got to school.

I felt alone in school. I went to my subjects as normal, but inside I was heading deeper and deeper into the darkness. Luckily for me, I found the only person who could help me get out of that tunnel: Sarah. Even in my darkest times, she could lift my spirits. Every time I saw her, I forgot about the bad things that happened and put myself back together. Sarah had become my safety blanket. She was like the training wheels on a bicycle that kept the bike from hitting the ground.

As the year went on, people still made fun of my jumping. When I wasn't with Sarah, I wished that I had some form of communication with her. I didn't have a mobile phone. But the communication I longed for didn't have to be a phone call, just some way for me to hear her voice, which always seemed to calm me down. I wish I had told Sarah what was going on inside my head, about the bullying and me jumping and the situation with the drum kit. Instead, I kept the whole mess inside.

I remember the first time I met Sarah's mother. Her name was Sally, a lovely woman. It was parents' evening at the school and I was with my mum. We somehow bumped into each other. I was so nervous, I had goosebumps. I didn't say much, just tried to make a good first impression with a friendly smile. I could tell Sarah was nervous too.

I introduced Sally and my mother, and Sally said that Sarah and I could exchange numbers to keep in contact with each other. Sarah and I exchanged glances and smiled. The only thing was that I didn't have a phone number to give. After that evening, my only thought was to buy a mobile phone, so I could keep in touch with Sarah.

Bean Bag Throwing: 2007

In an intense bean bag throwing final, I came in second. I looked down at my left hand, wondering what had given me trouble. Sarah saw me and, with her soft, gentle fingers, squeezed my left hand. "Listen to me," she said. "Don't worry about it. Remember that you came second place."

"Yes. At least I'm returning with a medal. I'll come back next year and do much better—I promise you, Sarah." I looked into her eyes while I spoke. I took my promises seriously. I didn't make them unless I planned to keep them, which was why I had only made a few in my lifetime.

"Can't wait to see that next year!" I swear she saw something in me at that moment. "Come on. Let's wait in the stands until they hand out the medals."

So we did. We went up to the stands and waited. Sarah updated me on her race. One of her friends called to her, and she walked up the stairs. I stayed on the lower grounds, watching the rest of the events. I was thinking and thinking of the promise I had just made. *I'm not going to fail on my promise.*

I received a gold medal for a race I had done earlier, in addition to the silver medal. All during the award ceremony, the only thought in my head was the promise I had made to Sarah. No matter what, I wasn't going to let her down.

5

Year Nine 2007–2008

I've got to be honest with you, my readers: my third and fourth years of school are a bit of a blur. I think it's because I was sinking into depression, without help from family or professionals to see what my mental state was like, how I was coping with being bullied at school, or if I was coping at all, for that matter.

You are probably thinking, "Where were his parents?"

Well, my father was a policeman, which meant that he wasn't home until very late, normally when my brother and I were asleep. Sometimes he wouldn't come home for two or three days. My mother was a highly qualified nurse. However, she had lost her job, which meant she was at home as my carer. She was in charge of feeding my brother and me, but for some reason she wouldn't cook anything. Most of the time we ate ready-made meals cooked in the microwave, like mini-pizzas from a supermarket. With Mum at home all the time, we stopped seeing our childminder, Max, which was very difficult. Saying goodbye to him for the last time was hard for me.

Fantasy Career Path

This was the year that I had to choose my GCSE subjects. This was scary as I did not know what I wanted to do with my life. Opportunities seemed few because of my cerebral palsy.

At lunchtime, I talked with Sarah about the coming year. I had no idea what I was doing. She was pretty confident that she would take drama as a GCSE. The very thought had me daydreaming that I was in a famous theatre, watching her perform the lead role in a massive play. The thought made me smile.

Then I snapped out of my dream to the realisation that I was wheeling into a heavy wooden fire door. I bumped into it with a big thump, pushing the door wide open. My chair wheels were almost spinning on the spot from the weight of the door. I kept moving forward, hoping that my wheels would catch a grip. They finally did. I made sure that I was holding the door for Sarah. She gave me a smile, appearing to be in disbelief of what had just happened, and said, "Thanks."

We went to the drama studio. Sarah introduced the teacher, Mrs Potter, to me since I had never met her before. Mrs Potter asked me if I was interested in taking drama as a GCSE subject. I thought my answer was a simple no, but then I took a sudden interest and asked some questions.

When I asked Mrs Potter about me being in a chair, and how it would affect me doing drama, she spent a few moments thinking. Then she came up with ideas of how to overcome the chair, and how she or someone would help me get on or off the stage. I was stunned by the positivity of the way that she came up with ideas. In my experience, that mindset was rare. I seriously considered ticking drama on the GCSE sheet that was due in a couple of months. I was going in hospital soon, so I needed to hand the sheet in before then.

Sarah and I were seeing each other more now. She came to my house frequently to hang out. It was great to watch TV with the one I loved so much for two to three hours, twice a week.

My mother seemed to fuss around more when Sarah was there. She would pop in every five minutes, asking if we wanted anything and if we were OK. At first I thought this was normal, but then it became worse. I quickly developed doubts that this was normal parenting behaviour.

When my World Changed Forever!

For my birthday, Sarah and I went to Pizza Hut. It was OK, but it would have been a lot better if my parents were not there, interrupting our conversation all the time.

As Valentine's Day approached, I got a text from Sarah, saying, *"I'm MAKING ur pressy now! Love u LOADS AND LOADS, Sarah Xxxxxxx."* Which kept my chin up, of course, knowing it was my first real Valentine's Day.

I was due to have an operation, and the day was getting nearer. Sarah kept my nerves at bay with another text: *"Hey, r u nervous? I would b! Txt me as soon as u come out of hospital, k? Love u Sarah xxx."*

The ninth of February soon came round, and I headed to hospital.

Here's the fancy medical language for what the surgeon was doing: *right supracondylar femoral extension/derotation + right derotation tibial osteotomy*. In simpler language, he made a 15 cm cut on my thigh and a 10 cm cut on my ankle, twisting the leg round and pulling to try to get it straight.

Father stayed with me until I was knocked out by the gas. When I woke, I couldn't feel anything from the hip down. It was the oddest feeling I have ever felt. Later I saw the doctor who supervised the operation. Dr Mark Paterson came down to see how I was. I told him I was feeling alright; however, I couldn't feel my legs. He explained that a needle had been put into my spinal cord, injecting a potent drug.

My first reaction to this information was, "But Doctor, how can I go toilet?"

Dr Paterson, the nurse, and my father all smiled. The doctor explained that because my entire lower body was paralysed, I was unlikely to toilet for a 'number two'. For urination, I was hooked up to a bag at the side of the bed. The nurse gently lifted the bag to show me. I thought it was a bit weird that I was now peeing in a plastic bag.

I spent nights just lying in bed, trying to enjoy the atmosphere of hospital at night. I had excellent staff looking after me, checking my pee bag to see if the colour and volume were normal, and making sure that I wasn't in any discomfort. Every day my parents came in to see me. They always brought me food, since hospital food is not the nicest in the world. Sometimes I got a visit from my grandparents, which was lovely. My granddad gave me a toy that I had always wanted, saying it was a late Christmas or a late birthday present.

But, while seeing family was great for support, I was missing Sarah.

A few days after the operation, on a typical morning, the nurses were doing their regular routine. Suddenly, my father got a phone call and headed outside. I assumed that it was work-related, because most of the time his calls were. Mother was helping me put my top on. I turned my head … and saw a familiar face.

Sarah was carrying her school bag and Father was carrying her coat. The first thought in my head was, *Oh no, I'm naked underneath the hospital robe, and I have a pee bag on the side of the bed!* I don't know why that was the first thing I thought of, but I was a bit uncomfortable. I checked and double checked that I was covered. Funny enough, the nurse was also checking, helped me tuck in any loose covers and being careful of the pee bag.

Sarah put her bag down by the guest chair. Watching her, I was nervous. Then she came over to me. I gave her the biggest hug and didn't want to let go. I had a huge grin on my face, warmth rushing through me. After I let go, she sat down on the chair at the side of the bed. She stayed for about an hour, asking questions like, "Did the operation go OK? When will they let you go home?"

While I tried to convince her that nothing had gone wrong, all I could think of was how great it was to see her. Someone accidentally knocked the pee bag. I jumped out of my skin in shock.

"Oh my God! Are you OK? What's the matter?" Sarah said.

I squealed, "Never felt better!" Then I cracked up with laughter.

Sarah gave me a worried smile. There's nothing on this planet that can describe how it feels to have someone care so much for you at a time when you really need them.

When the nurse finished checking up on me, my father grabbed his camera and told Sarah and I to get as close as possible. This was a bit difficult to do while I had no feelings in my legs. The best I could do was move my head and shoulders as far left as possible. My father snapped away. At one point, Mother said, "Tom, go on, hold her hand then!" I looked at Sarah and held my left hand out, palm open, welcoming Sarah to place our hands together. We turned to the camera and smiled.

The picture below is my favourite of all time.

For privacy reasons, I had to crop the photo, which is a shame. It would have been nice for you to see how happy we both were. I hope that at least you can see how pleased I was with a person who brought me so much happiness.

After about a hundred photos (sometimes my father can get carried away), it was time for Sarah to head off home. I was deeply sad because I didn't know when I would see her again. She gave me another warm hug, and I didn't want to let go. I said, "When I get back home, I will give you a text or ring."

She smiled and got her bag while my father got her coat. Mother said, "Tom, are you going to kiss her goodbye?"

I felt my cheeks go super-hot and probably bright red. I looked over to Sarah, and she was just as embarrassed as me. I can't speak on Sarah's behalf, of course, but I was thoroughly embarrassed. All I could think was, *I can't have my first kiss with Sarah while I'm in hospital and both my parents are watching me!* I think I was waiting for the perfect moment for us to have our first kiss.

After the most awkward pause of my life, we said our goodbyes. I watched Sarah walk to the exit, as I tried to figure out what had just happened. Also, I wondered, was she thinking the same thing?

* * * * *

After that day with Sarah, the rest of my recovery was painfully slow. I gradually got some feeling back in my lower body, beginning with my feet. It was almost like a scene in *Kill Bill*. (If you watch the film, you'll know what scene I'm talking about.) The pain slowly crept up on me as the effects of the painkillers wore off.

The worst thing was that I hadn't had a 'number two' for a couple of days. To trick my body into it, a nurse had to stick something up there. I can't think of the name of it. But it was not a pleasurable experience, I can tell you!

Moving on from that thought.

After what seemed to be a lifetime, the day came for me to leave hospital. I was very happy to go home, mainly because I could contact Sarah again.

On 13 February, I received a text from Sarah. She asked for my home address, as she was going to send me a 'pressy'. My mind was racing after she texted me; I was over the moon. I went to sleep early because I just couldn't wait for Valentine's Day.

The next day I woke up and immediately thought that today was 14th February, which meant it was Valentine's Day! Soon after I ate breakfast, I got a text from Sarah: *"Hi here's a Valentine's rose! @)>-% --- love u! Guess! Lol."*

I was ecstatic. Having my first-ever Valentine's Day with someone to share it with meant a lot to me. When you have strong feelings for another person, you should treat every moment that you have with them like a Valentine's Day.

Sarah followed up with another text, asking if I had received her 'pressy' in the post. Unfortunately, I hadn't, which I was a little sad about.

A few days passed. One afternoon, Mother brought in the mail. My eagle eyes were on her hands as she walked towards me. She gave me an envelope. On the top, it read S.W.A.L.K. I wasn't sure what this meant. Before I could read any more, Mother asked, "Do you know what S.W.A.L.K means?" I shook my head. She pointed to each letter as she recited each word:

"Sealed With A Loving Kiss."

Then I read the letter inside this intriguing envelope. I felt positive energy flooding my body like water pouring into a glass. When the joy overflowed, I felt the emotions leak out from my eyes. I couldn't believe that another person had such feelings of love for me. I could almost hear Sarah's voice reading her words out loud, as if she were in the room.

I heard a noise that sounded like Father was starting to cook dinner, and this snapped me back to reality. I tried to rein in my emotions. I wiped my face clean of the happy tears. I quickly put the letter in the envelope and hid it. I acted like everything was normal.

Just before dinner, I couldn't control myself. I got my phone and texted Sarah: *"I got your pressy. Thank you for the lovely card."*

She replied, *"Here's another rose: @)>-% --- Love Sarah xxx."*

I soon found out that having a mobile phone and a lack of social skills could be very destructive in a relationship.

A few months later, Sarah had a party. My leg was still in plaster, so it was with great difficulty that I could get about and mingle, but Father took me to her party. I wanted to make a very good impression with her family, but I had limited social skills. Looking back, I realise how hard it was for Sarah to involve me in discussions, because I was lost for words. I was always with my family and did not have any experience of mixing with people I didn't know.

I just love the drawing at the bottom my leg. So funny!

My recovery was slow and long. Every day brought the same routine. I slowly slipped into a dark place. I don't know how to explain this, but while it was happening, I kept getting a shiver down my spine. I felt super weird, almost as if the whole world were suddenly on top of my shoulders. I knew something wasn't right. I didn't know exactly what to think about the funny feeling, nor did I understand what it was trying to tell me.

I was texting Sarah almost every hour of every day as I tried to cope. I was acutely aware of how dependent on others I was, and how I couldn't really do much on my own. How could I look after other people if I couldn't look after myself?

Needless to say, it ended up too much for her.

One day, I had a very bad feeling. This proved itself accurate as I got a series of text messages which told me that my relationship was over. As soon as the last text came, I closed my phone and gently placed it down. I went to bed and pulled the covers over my shoulders as if I were about to go to sleep. I leaned my head to the left, resting it on the pillow, and very slowly closed my eyes. I breathed in deeply until my lungs were full. In what felt like the slowest exhale ever, I breathed out of my nose, releasing any sort of regret or need to bust out sobbing.

With my eyelids closed and relaxed, I could feel something wet running down. It followed my cheekbone all the way to my neck, followed by another and another. I didn't have the strength to wipe my face. I just lay there, letting the tears run down while I told myself that it was over now.

I only wish that I had had someone to talk to at this dark time. I felt that I couldn't tell my parents; they were busy with their own lives, and they didn't ask or understand what I was going through. My mum in particular was very distant and unapproachable. Something was happening to her, and I wasn't aware of it at the time.

The day came when I had to go back to school. I didn't know how to feel, so I went through the morning just as normal. On the bus, everyone took an interest in my operation and asked endless questions. Before I knew it, we were at school. I knew that I would bump into Sarah sooner or later, and I was dreading it.

After lunch, I saw Sarah. She made it clear our relationship was over. I tried to speak, but no words came out. I quickly glanced at her eyes and finally said, "Yes." Then I bolted away as fast as possible.

I couldn't believe how much our friendship had changed. For a few weeks, I was talking to a partner. Then, in a heartbeat, she became a stranger to me.

As the weeks went on, I tried to adjust to the fact that I was alone, with no one to connect with or call a friend. I felt like I was in outer space, drifting away into the unknown. I know I went through my regular school days. However, I was in my own world, in the darkest place, and nothing around me mattered any more.

On 16th March, I tried just talking to Sarah again. It didn't go so well. I believe that was the last time I texted her. I knew then that I had lost my friend for sure. The relationship had shattered into a billion pieces. I was heartbroken.

The rest of the year I don't remember very well. I was floating into the blackness of space. I made every effort not to run into Sarah, so I wouldn't end up freezing and staring at her. I went to the drama teacher and told her that I wasn't going to choose the subject for GCSE. She was disappointed. I explained that without Sarah at my side, I couldn't do drama.

Sometimes I couldn't help myself; my eyes would be tempted to look at her, and my mind wondered, *Why? Why did it have to end the way it did?* Then Sarah would tell me off for staring at her. I became extremely nervous around her, to the point where I couldn't look at or talk to her. Seeing her close triggered my 'flight or freeze' response—usually both at the same time.

Sometimes Sarah seemed to be looking at me. She would give the biggest smile and shrug. She was so happy. Then she'd walked past me to sit down, still smiling and chatting away. I was pleased that she was smiling and happy, and I wished I could feel the same. But however hard I tried to be happy, I could not be.

The darkness grew bigger and more significant. It consumed my mind like thick smoke going round and round and round endlessly.

6

Year Ten: 2008–2009

I was very unhappy at this time of the life.

When summer came, I spent the majority of the summer holidays playing video games and watching the latest TV programmes, attempting to forget everything about school. As the holiday drew closer to ending, it became harder to find ways of escaping. I had never felt so alone in my fifteen years. I had family around me, so I was not entirely isolated. But, then as now, I had no deep connection with any of my family members. When they visited or when I visited them, I put on a mask to hide my despair and depressed state of mind.

I must have been a good actor. Not one of my family members knew how depressed I was, to my knowledge anyway.

During the day, escape was easier. However, during the evening, my mind was crowded with a million different thoughts. To this day I have trouble falling into a deep sleep, but when I do, like many of us, I have dreams. Most of the time when I awake, I have forgotten the details of those dreams. Twice, this wasn't the case. After all these years, I still remember them vividly.

Dream Number 1

One night before I went to sleep, I opened my drawer and searched. I came across a plastic sleeve. I gently took hold of the edge to have a look. Inside was an envelope. It was my Valentine's Day gift from Sarah. I took out the letter, and a small, handmade pink photo frame fell out onto my lap. I picked it up, and I was looking at the beautiful face of Sarah. My mind started racing again.

After a minute or so, I put the picture down to one side. I proceeded to open the yellow letter and read. I felt guilt within me, and my heart rate rose. My hands were sweaty, I wiped them on my shirt.

I put the letter and the picture back into the envelope and placed it in the bottom drawer of my bedside table. Then I tried to go to sleep. The next morning, I slowly woke up after hearing noises that meant the rest of the family were getting up. I stayed in bed, lying on my back, staring at the ceiling, remembering what I had seen inside my own head and wondering what it meant.

It started with a quick glimpse of me walking up a royal-blue set of stairs. The image quickly flashed white, and I was now standing in the bathroom. It had white walls to the ceiling with a layer tiles above the bath. The standard-sized bath was very near to filling up with water, from which gentle steam rose. When it seemed like enough water, I reached over and turned the taps off. I lifted my right foot and placed it on my left knee for support, then started to take off my sock.

I didn't hear Sarah walking up the stairs. She must have turned left at the top of the stairs, because suddenly there she was at the door to the bathroom. She was wearing a black polo shirt and some sort of bottoms, her hair tied back into a ponytail.

I was terrified when I realised she was standing in the doorway. I took a sharp breath in, my eyes wide as they could possibly be. I quickly covered myself up with both hands. She smiled and calmly said, "Aww, don't worry. I've seen it. You can relax."

A bit taken aback by how calm she was, I shifted my hands, now feeling relaxed and calm. I put my right hand on the top of the bath for support and leaned over the tub to put my left hand in the water, moving it in a circling motion. The water was the right temperature, and I climbed in. I leaned back to let the water cover me like a blanket.

Still watching me, Sarah walked towards the bathtub. It appeared she had decided to climb in, though she was fully clothed. When I realised what she was about to do, I quickly sat up. Somehow we both managed to fit in side by side, which still puzzles me.

So there I was, sitting crossed-legged in the bathtub, and in front of me is the most beautiful woman in the world, smiling. I could look at that smile all day.

After gazing into her eyes for a moment, I leaned forward to kiss her. She closed her eyes and copied my actions. We both edged forward, and just inches away from her lips, I …

… suddenly woke up!

My first thoughts were of disbelief at what I had just seen. I desperately tried to fall back into a deep sleep and see what would happen the moment that our lips touched. I shut my eyes again and again. Each time I tried to tighten them more, so keen was I to fall back to sleep. After a few tries, though, I gave up. I just couldn't do it. I was disappointed with myself.

I ended up lying sideways, wide awake. My mind raced at a hundred miles per hour as I sought to remember every detail of my dream. It must have worked.

Shortly after that day, it was time to go to school again. I was dreading it after being bullied and losing my only friend. I stayed calm until one day in the medical centre, when someone came up to see if I was all right. That made it clear that my disappointment was starting to show. For the first time, I decided to open up. I told her details of the dream described above.

I was just filling in the details when Sarah walked into the room. As soon I saw her, I froze. My mind screamed at me, *I need to get out of this room!*

Sarah left, and I resumed talking to the other girl. To make it worse, Sarah returned and firmly said, "I know that you are talking about me."

My head was truly messed up. I felt something wasn't the same with me after that day. I was slowly turning into a different person. I wasn't the passionate, confident person I had been when I started high school.

Many other factors caused the change in my behaviour. One of them was how people gossiped about what I said to Sarah, and it wasn't a few people either. They made comments to me like, "Did you really say …?" That didn't help my mindset. I knew my words were often wrong. I just wanted to brush it off and finish the year.

* ✳ ✳ ✳ *

In a year, the school had three or four terms, The first half of each term was spent getting used to the new subjects, new classrooms, and new teachers. For me, there was also learning the new LSAs' timetable. I'd chosen business studies, food tech, history, maths, English, and science.

In the second term, I found a person who had similar interests, and we became friends. His name was Andrew. During that year and the next, we talked during lunchtimes. Occasionally he came to my house, and we would hang out, playing computer games or card games. It felt good to finally have a friend to talk to after being so alone for what seemed like years.

Through Andrew, I met one of his mates, a boy called Jack who was a bit of a chatterbox. The three of us hung out pretty much every lunchtime. We went around the school, causing a little bit of trouble here and there.

I started forgetting who I was. I didn't notice myself changing into a whole new person: sarcastic, witty, short-tempered, and foul-mouthed. That was the worst one for me personally: I swore without thinking. If you had asked me at the start of high school if I would ever swear, I would have said, "No, there's no need for swearing." I'm scared to think back and realise how little I cared about anything—not just school, but my relationships with people.

This carried over to the third and fourth terms of the year. I even had a go at some teachers and LSAs. One of my worst moments, I think, was in maths. I was sitting in the back of the class with an LSA. The person sitting next to me happened to be the rudest girl in the whole year. Halfway through the lesson, she got on my nerves to the point that I said, "Can you kindly shut it, please?"

She replied, "*You* can shut it."

There we were, going back and forth, which got the LSA annoyed. The girl then yelled, "Shut the f— up!" Without even thinking, I dropped the F-word back at her.

Which wasn't me at all.

It shocked me how fast I said it, like an automatic response. How I didn't get in trouble that day, I do not know.

During this dark time, while I was having these breakdowns, there was one person who helped me. She happened to be my form tutor for the two years of GCSEs, Ms Papadopoulos. She was only about five feet tall—or perhaps she just seemed short because nearly everyone from my year group was a foot taller than she. Her hair was black and cut just below the shoulders. She had a very positive attitude and always had a smile on her face—but she could control the class when necessary. The best thing about her was that she was easy to talk to.

I played basketball outside of school every Friday evening. I took the training seriously. So I was thinking of ways to put in more training time, as I wanted to improve as much as possible. Sure, I could work on my game at home. I had an eight-foot hoop in my driveway with which to practise my shooting skills. That was all good, but I wanted more.

One day I found Ms Papadopoulos in a class. I went up to her, and we started chatting. "How's life at home?" she asked. "How are you finding things at school?" We ended up with me saying that I needed to put in more basketball practice. She said, "Have you tried asking the PE teachers for access to the gym or sports hall?"

I said, "No, I haven't. I don't know if they will listen to me."

"Give it a shot. You never know unless you try," she replied.

It took another week or two before I found it in me to go to the PE teachers' quarters. After a few attempts of turning up and finding no one, I finally saw two PE teachers sitting there: Mrs Brooks and Mr Roberts. I parked my chair in the door and placed my hands on either side of the door frame.

"Hi, Tom boy! How it's going?" Mr Roberts greeted me.

"I'm fine," I said.

Mrs Brooks said, "Good! What can we do for you?"

"I … I … I wanted to ask you i-if it was pos … pos … possible to have access to the gym or sports hall?"

At first, both of them seem a bit taken back from my request. "Ummm," hedged Mrs Brooks. "Any particular reason?"

"Well … I've got this big competition coming up, and I would like to put in the practice whenever I can, to improve my skills, so I am ready for action when it comes to the tournament." That was the best explanation I could think of on the spot.

Just as she began her response, I heard, "Pardon me, Tommo." I moved away from the doorway to let a third teacher inside the small office. "What's going on here, then?"

"Tom just asked if he can have access to the gym or sports hall, so he can practise for a tournament," Mrs Brooks said.

The newcomer gave a little "hmm" in response.

Mr Roberts said, "Unfortunately, that has to be a no, Tom. We can't let you use the gym without some form of adult supervision."

I had known that the chances of my request being granted were highly unlikely. But I am not going to lie: I really had been hoping that this crazy idea was somehow going to work. Disappointment filled me up.

Mrs Brooks shrugged and gave me a sad smile. "Sorry."

Afterwards, the conversation became a bit happier. All three teachers talked about my competition. They reminisced about my year eight sports day and the epic showdown at the finals of the bean bag match. That did brighten my spirits.

If you don't ask, you'll never know the answer. That was what I learned. Sadly, I am still not very good at asking for things.

A week or so passed before I spoke to Ms Papadopoulos again. I told her about how the conversation had gone with the PE department. As I talked, I started to think about what changes I could make to the school that would affect the disability community as a whole, rather than just myself. For example, there were only one or two clubs that focused on students with disabilities.

Ms Papadopoulos suggested that I write a letter to the new head teacher, Ms Smith. So I did. Looking back, that first letter was definitely focused on myself. However, it got her attention. She wrote back that I should get people to sign a petition to show that other students were of the same mindset.

This was a bit of a blow to me, because unless I had to, I didn't engage in conversation with my peers. Unfortunately too, I started this campaign very late in the year, and my mock exams were coming up. I had to push everything off until the next year.

Dream Number 2

A few days before GCSE mocks, I had a second dream that still puzzles me. In it, I was walking towards the school sports field with a football in hand. I was among a bunch of people whom I didn't recognise. I held the ball in front of me and set up for a kick. The people who were with me ran ahead. I gave the ball a massive boot and it really flew.

Flash out of that scene to me doing skill moves with the ball to pass an opponent. I outskilled him and made him trip over his own feet. I looped the ball towards my teammate. After helping my opponent to his feet, I gave him a pat on the shoulder. He ran off to help his defence. I stood there, hands on my knees, catching my breath. I grabbed a nearby towel and wiped the sweat from my forehead.

Something caught my attention from the corner of my vision. From a distance, it looked like a blur of shadow. I dropped the towel on a pile of school jackets being used as goals. When I looked back at the dark blur, I could faintly see the details. It was only a few meters away from me. It turned out to be Sarah walking towards me.

As soon as I realised it was her, I was a bit unsure what to make of it. The closer she got, the more uneasy I felt. When Sarah was only a few feet away, I tried to step back, but immediately she was right in front of me. I could feel the air that she was exhaling. She placed her hands on my shoulders, and her hand came towards me. She gave me a quick peck on the lips. Then she slowly turned away to her left, smiling, to start heading back.

It all happened very fast. I stood looking very confused. I'd forgotten entirely that there was a game going on behind me. As she turned away from me, I found my tongue and managed to say, "I … I … I don't understand? Why did you just kiss me?"

She briefly stopped in her tracks. With a shrug, she replied, "I don't know." Her cheeks turning a little reddish. "I just felt like kissing you," she added softly. Then she fully turned away with a hop in her step and returned to the group of shadows. It must have been her group of friends.

I heard from a distance, "Heads up, Tom!" When I turned towards the voice, a blur was coming right towards my nose. I raised my hands to protect my face and I woke up.

I was out of breath. I sat up in my bed, sweat dripping down my nose. I had thought the ball was going to smash my nose in.

It was an experience similar to dream number 1: waking up in the early morning and thinking about what I had just seen. I kept on thinking this time. The dream had shown me on my feet again, playing football with a group of people who seemed to be my friends. This dream was different because I saw a kiss actually happen. I didn't know how to react to that. I knew it was only a dream, but what did it mean? What was my brain trying to communicate to me? Or was it trying to mess me up with false conclusions?

That made two dreams in which I had been on my feet. I seemed to be in a happy, healthy place in my life. However, in each dream I was a bit confused about the situation.

To this day I don't fully understand these two dreams or why they have stuck with me for so long inside the complex of my mind and heart.

Hydrotherapy: Aquatic Physiotherapy

I think it must have been a year after the break-up with Sarah when I was asked to try out hydrotherapy. This basically meant physio lessons using water to change things up a bit. At first, I turned down the offer, because my gut feeling about water was a bit shaky. However, I decided to give it a try after the school physio said that the therapists would stick by my side most of way while I was in the water.

My mother drove me to the place. We parked and walked into the building. We were greeted by the physio, who briefly gave me a summary of what was going to happen. He made sure that I was all right with what they were planning. I proceeded into the disabled changing rooms, put on some swim trunks, and jumped into the pool! OK, not really. I waited for one of the physios to slowly lower me into the pool. Mother sat on a bench, watching me the whole time. Not going to lie, sometimes it felt very creepy knowing that another person was staring at me for a length of time. This was the routine while I did the hydrotherapy for a couple of weeks.

I can't remember exactly what type of exercises I did in the pool. I think mostly they were general swimming movements for the backstroke and butterfly stroke. I moved my hips and legs in ways I wasn't used to, since I didn't do much walking. After my operations, my legs hadn't fully been the same as they once were. The hydrotherapy was designed to put them in the right places. Everyone at this point was trying their hardest to get me walking.

No one had told me that Sarah was doing hydrotherapy as well. "Why does it matter to you if Sarah's there?" I hear you saying. Well, if I had known she was going to be there, I most likely wouldn't have gone. That's not a good enough explanation? Fine. I was a total wreck! I couldn't talk to her. I was unable to stay calm when we were only a few feet apart.

There were times, taking a short break, when I was left on my own resting on one of the corners of the pool. That in itself made me a bit nervous because I'm not always steady in the water. I tried to keep my feet on the bottom of the pool and my arms on either side of the corner edge.

One of these times, I was scanning the pool, looking for one of the physios. From the corner of my vision, I saw Sarah swim by from left to right. She was only a few feet away. I could have reached out and my fingertips would have touched her. I went from a little nervous to having a mini panic attack. It was a miracle that I stayed on my feet.

I had a small flashback to an episode when I sat on the edge of a pool float and my friend jumped on the other side of the same float. The impact sent me flying into the water, where I was as helpless as a turtle on its back, until the same friend helped me to the side of the side of the pool. I do not know how, but that flashback helped me to regain my balance. However, my heart rate was out of control.

What made the whole situation worse was that on the benches, I saw Mother waving her hands around, urging me to splash water on Sarah! I just stared at her and shook my head. Mother didn't get the message, persisting with her gestures. She was disappointed that I didn't push water Sarah's way.

I'm not sure if it was the same day or sometime during the following weeks, but I was waiting in the corridor when a man walked towards me and started talking to me. He was Sarah's granddad! When I realised who

I was talking to, I felt uneasy and light-headed. Apart from Sally, Sarah's mother, I hadn't spoken to any of Sarah's family members. I just assumed that any of them would now hate my guts.

Many thoughts were in my head all at once: *Does he know that my relationship with Sarah ended? Is he going to give me the 'man talk' about looking after his grandchild? Or is he going to give me the 'how dare you treat a lady the way that you did' speech?* As you can tell, I was basing my fears on what I had seen on TV.

I was totally wrong. He spoke in a friendly manner, and I felt at ease immediately. I don't remember the full context of the talk, but at the end, he then asked me if I was willing to attend a summer party with his family. I was uncomfortable with this offer, and I couldn't give him a straight answer. He realised that I was struggling to give him an answer, so he smiled and said, "Don't worry, you don't have to say at this minute. The offer is still open if you choose it."

I felt super embarrassed. My intention had been to give this man the impression that I was friendly, reliable, and confident. But I guess I must have looked tiny, dependent, and weak. After that, we went our separate ways.

From what I had seen, I'd always liked Sarah's family. They were very different from my own. They talked and acted as if I were just another person. They didn't use the sugar-coated baby talk, all talking to the chair and not the person, that my family and so many people did so often.

Mock Exams

Very quickly the mock exams arrived. These were taken mostly by people with disabilities and other kids who were predicted to get low-end grades. We were told to go to a large classroom with enough chairs for fifteen students. At the back were some really tiny rooms, enough for a table and two chairs. These were for the students who needed an LSA to write for them. Once assigned to a room, the student used it for the rest of the day. On the right side of the classroom was a row of windows, and one of the tiny rooms had one a window as well. None of us wanted that room: it would get stuffy and hot really fast.

I just flew through the questions with at least twenty minutes to spare. Then I had to sit in the room until the official time was done. I could hardly stand it, sitting there in silence for that length of time. When the time was up, I was free to leave the room and ring up Mother to pick me up. This scenario repeated until the exams were finished and the summer holidays began.

That was it for year ten. I know it's short, but that's because in my fourth year not much actually happened. Due to me being in a dark place, I didn't pay any attention to what was going on around me, nor did I care. Year ten, in a nutshell, is always a build-up for GCSEs that happen in year eleven.

7

Year Eleven 2009–2010

Year eleven is officially the last year of high school. It's the year of the massive GCSEs that determine one's future—well, that's what the teacher reminded us almost daily.

Over the summer holidays I had calmed down a bit. I wasn't as angry with the world as I had been. That doesn't mean I was jumping with joy and singing in the streets about how great my life was. One day my school report came in the post, and my parents gave it to me to read. Almost every teacher had said the same things: "Tom at most times refuses to do any work in class. The homework that was handed in was at a poor standard. There were times of rudeness to other members of staff."

Afterwards, I gave it to my father so he could have a look for himself. He came back and tried to make it sound positive, but I didn't believe him. I never found out what he honestly thought of my report.

Seeing what the teachers were saying did disappoint me a little bit. I realised I was becoming the type of person I feared the most.

When school started, I was struggling to compose my frustration with my feelings for Sarah. One way I tried to project my energy was on paper. Here is one of my many attempts to be the great William Shakespeare. So I can amuse myself with my embarrassment of sharing my English talent. firstly is a poem. I'm not sure if you can call it a poem. Anyhow, I wrote this on 22 January 2011:

I miss you
Maybe it wasn't meant to happen
It should be the present not the past
I only realise that now, as I'm getting older and wiser
I wish that you were still in my life
Maybe I as a person would change for the better, not for the worst
A happy soul, not a lonely soul
Maybe go out a bit more with no one else watching over us

I Love You
By Thomas Kandiah

My bedroom in our house in London was downstairs, between the staircase and the living room—which meant there was heavy foot traffic through my room. I tried to write these on my computer while hiding them from anyone passing by. It was a bit funny really, pouring my heart out onto the page while making sure no one caught me.

I wrote a letter on 26 March 2011, trying to explain everything to Sarah.

Dear Sarah,

I am having trouble telling you this, and every time our paths cross, I automatically go in the opposite direction. So I decided to write it up instead.

I don't know why not, but after two years of you getting tired of me trying to get us together, leading to you shouting at me and telling people to make me stop, I still have very strong feelings for you. I think you should know the truth behind why I did what I did.

Do you remember when I had that operation on both of my legs? Every Monday, we used to watch 'Genie in the House' for half an hour. Mum would check up on us every two minutes.

That was the reason, because we weren't alone for the time we were together. This lowered my confidence to talk to you, and I had a feeling that the relationship wasn't working out.

I know what you might be thinking: that I should have come to you and we might have been able to sort it out, right?

But I didn't because I was dumb and stupid back then and you were my only friend. I had no hobbies. So all my attention was on you. I'm not sure if that's a good thing or not.

Instead of telling you that I felt it wasn't working out, which might hurt you, I chose to make you break us up so I would be hurt instead. I'd rather be hurt instead of you. All I want is you to be happy.

But things could be different this time. I have more friends now. I have taken up wheelchair basketball and archery.

So far the year of 2011 has been a good one, but there's someone missing in my heart. And that someone is you, Sarah.

Trust me when I say I tried to move on and find a new soul mate. But I don't feel the same way as I felt back when I first saw you. That feeling I still have to this day.

I'm not sure if this helps, but I kept the Valentine's Day card that you gave to me on our first Valentine's Day together. I now know that I should have sent you some flowers or something, to show that I cared. I didn't understand what it takes to be a boyfriend then, but I have a better understanding now.

Yours faithfully
Thomas

Award Ceremony

A few weeks later, the school hosted another award ceremony, and I was invited. It was my last one. It happened in the main hall. The main hall hadn't changed much since the previous time I'd been there.

I turned up a bit early again. When I wheeled through the doors, the floor of the hall was a shiny, dark brown colour. I had to navigate through a narrow gap between two groups of chairs, where all the parents would sit to watch the event. At the end of this seating was quite a bit of room. The teachers were running around, making sure everything was set up right.

In the front of the hall was a large platform. On top of it were two huge banners with photos of students doing events, slightly changed from last time I was here. At the middle of the stage was a microphone resting on a stand and two stools on either side. Behind the stools was a huge, blank projector screen. The bottom edge was almost touching the wooden flooring of the stage. Right above the parents' chairs was the projector box, its big lens staring at the blank screen.

There was a single row of chairs, roughly fifteen of them, where the teachers would sit during the evening. About twelve chairs down, at the side of the stage, was a tiny table with a small laptop on it. The laptop seemed to be connected to the projector screen. Behind the laptop setup was a single desk. Two of the teachers were filling it up with trophies and medals of all sorts, in some form of grouping system.

To the left of the stage was a small grid of chairs, perhaps seven by seven. These were the seats that students would sit in, waiting until their names were called. Then they would get up and walk to the stage to receive their medal or trophy from the head of the school.

One of the teachers told me that they had left a space for me to park myself for the ceremony. I went there immediately and watched the set-up take place. Soon more students came in, and parents began taking seats. It was about half six when the organisers started playing music. Then we watched the head teacher walk to the stage with someone else—a book author; I wish I could remember who. They reached the stage, and the head teacher sat down. Now the evening could begin.

There was a buzz in the room, with parents, teachers, and students all chatting among themselves. When the head teacher stood again and walked up to the microphone, the whole hall fell silent. When the head spoke, we all felt we had to listen to every word.

"Morning, everyone. So here we are again: another award ceremony to see these inspiring students and give them a reward for the efforts they have given to this school. I'm so glad to see some new, talented faces, and also some familiar faces here with us tonight. It pleases me that these students kept up the hard work and set an example for generations to come …"

I felt slightly sad when he said this. It got me thinking of the way I had acted in the last year or two. I was by no means inspiring, nor a great example to the younger generations that might be inclined to look up to me.

"…This night is particularly special to me because tonight will be my last time hosting the award ceremony. So let's make tonight a really special one that we will remember for days to come."

Once he finished, he gave a tiny bow and returned to his seat. Everyone clapped. A teacher walked up to the small table at the side of the stage. The clapping died out as soon as he started talking.

One after another, teachers gave out speeches about their students and their respective subjects. I sat in my parking spot wondering why I had been asked to come to this ceremony. I was happy to be there, but the teachers I had spoken to about it beforehand were quick to change the subject. So I had no idea what type of reward I was receiving. Which I guess was exciting. I was also wondering because this was my GCSE year. The previous year, the teachers had told me that I would spend the year revising for mock exams—there were no awards for *that*.

In the end, I decided to wait and see. There was no need to worry or overthink it. Worry would spoil the moment when it was my turn to go up.

It wasn't too long until my name was called. Here's roughly how the teacher's speech went: "Our next student has truly been a role model, from getting third place in his first youth games to the epic battle for the gold in 2007, when he sadly came second. His athletic accomplishments were truly something special, and he has made many more memories since."

The teacher glanced up and met my eyes amid the crowd of students. We smiled; it seemed we were both remembering the conclusion of the final. Then she looked down at her paper and continued. "Each time, he showed off his skill to overcome whatever difficulties he had to face, accomplishing so much in the process. He has been a truly inspiring figure for all of us, not only his peers. I speak on behalf of all of us when I say that we hope you continue to show the same effort when facing the challenges waiting for you in the future. Which is why we decided to reward Thomas with this wonderful trophy for courage."

During the speech, the head of the school and his guest had made their way down the steps to stand just in front of the stage. It took me a moment or two to get myself together. I hadn't expected an award for inspiring people at all. A voice to my right, that of a teacher, encouraged me to move forward. I might have appeared a bit lost for a split second, but now, with two hands on my wheels, I moved forward. I told myself to remain calm and keep my chair going smoothly in front of the crowd.

When I finally reached the front, I first greeted the head teacher with a good handshake. He said, "Well done, Thomas."

I could only give a smile and a slight whisper, "Thank you." I was not even sure if he heard me.

After that, I was greeted by the special guest. The author was holding something that at first I couldn't recognise. *No time to start thinking about the prize. Focus on shaking hands and smile*, I told myself. I saw it as a blue blur. I smiled as I received the prize, then turned my chair to face the parents. I felt hands on both of my shoulders that I presumed were those of the head and the guest. I waited, watching everyone clapping away. It only lasted about two minutes, but felt much longer. I scanned the hall and gave the nod to any teachers I saw.

I was delighted to receive this trophy. Back in my parking spot, I looked at it for a minute or two. Then I placed it on my lap and let it rest while I enjoyed the rest of the evening. Later, I had a proper look at the blue-tinted glass trophy. It had a petal border surrounding a pure white circle in the centre, with blue text within that read:

Mayfield
SSCO
School Sports Partnership

Near the bottom, there was a golden rectangle plate, and the text said:

Partnership Olympic Awards
Courage

As I continued listening to the teachers talk and watching other students go up, I thought about the presentation speech the teacher had given me. As I was thinking, that teacher got up to the stand and started to speak again. I didn't realise it was me that they were talking about until the very end, when my name was called out. OK, there were hints that I could have picked up on. However, my head was already full up with all sorts of thoughts. My brain was too busy.

I only heard the last line of the speech: "And that's why we have decided to give Tom a surprise award, that he had no idea till now, for his work to inspire our younger generation. Tom has shown them that if you put your mind to the task, you can achieve just about anything! So I welcome back up to the front, Thomas Kandiah!"

I couldn't believe what I was hearing. It was unbelievable to think that I had had an impact on the younger students of the school. The last word that came to my mind to describe myself was "inspiring".

The head teacher and the guest headed down the stage once more. I wasn't as nervous to go up this time. Don't get me wrong: I was still anxious and confused. I had a little trouble pushing my chair. Maybe I was trying to rush. The head teacher said, "Take your time. We'll all wait for you." This really helped me.

When I finally got up to the front, I did the same thing as before. I shook the head teacher's hand and the guest's hand with a tiny bow. I turned to face the parents and saw my father dancing round with his camera. I nodded to the teacher who had presented me, then headed back to my parking spot.

Parked once more, I had a proper look at the stony square that I had just got. It had a glossy texture and polished feel to it. The light bounced off it. It had Greek or Roman leaves in the middle, surrounding a pure white circle in the centre. Blue text read:

Mayfield
SSCO
School Sports Partnership

Under the golden leaves was a golden rectangle plate, which read:

OLYMPIC AWARDS 2010
INSPIRATION

49

Before long, the night was over, and the students met up with their parents to show off their prizes. I did the same. As we were setting off back home, we were stopped by a couple of teachers—not all at once, of course—and each shook my hand, saying things like, "Congratulations, Tom" and "Well done, Tom". After speaking to me, they turned to my parents to have a brief talk. As they chit-chatted, I stared at the blank wall or watched teachers stacking chairs.

When the night was over, it was back to ordinary school life—which meant revision classes. *Oh great! Looking forward to them!*

Granddad

I can't remember exactly when, but it was before prom and GCSEs when my granddad got ill and was brought to hospital. My brother and I visited him sometimes on the weekends or after school. I heard many stories of the type of person my granddad was. They didn't change my view of the man.

A few years back, when both my parents were working long hours, granddad would be at the house when my school bus dropped me off after school. He helped me to walk into the house (the house I grew up in had a massive step before the door). Honestly, it was probably not the smartest thing to do, having someone in their late fifties or early sixties help a kid up the step. We managed it, but it sometimes got me scared. If I had fallen, I might have taken Granddad down with me. I wasn't worried about me, a fit 15-year-old. A fall was no big deal for me. But for a 60-year-old, a lot of things may go wrong.

What I liked about the man was that, once inside the house, he would actually take the time to help me. He got me out of my coat and blazer, offered me a drink if I wanted one, and waited until I was all sorted before he headed off to collect my brother from his school. It sounds like such a simple thing to do, right? Well, not for most of my family members.

Here's an example for you. When Mother had to leave her job, she became my carer. She was at home every day, so there was no need for Granddad to come. When I got off the bus, Mother was waiting for me to bring me in. I admit this part of the arrangement was more comfortable most of the time; probably she was twenty years younger than my granddad. But if my bus was late or I was in the middle of taking off my school uniform, and it was time to collect my brother from school, Mother would just leave.

This could mean that she would leave me tangled up with my coat in the middle of the room, helpless as a new puppy. I could try to finish on my own, but in cases where it was too difficult, I simply sat there in a tangle till she came back with my brother.

Or let's say that my bus turned up late or broke down. When I did finally get to my house, Mother would be standing there as normal. She would help me in, then carry my chair in—and then leave me at the stairs and rush to collect my brother. This happened almost every time I was late to get home.

One day it went to the extreme. I was surprised that I didn't flip out. As always, I got home, and once inside the house, I wanted to go upstairs for some reason. (I could go up the set of stairs that we had in that house, but I needed some help.) There were fourteen steps on the inside staircase. Mother was helping me, and at about the sixth or seventh stair, her phone went off. As if she had totally forgotten how unstable I was, she went down the steps to answer it. The caller was my brother, asking for a lift home. So she put on her coat and left the house—leaving me *halfway up the stairs*!

So Granddad got sick and was sent to the hospital. I had to deal with my school life (which was hard enough as it was) and with life going on at home. My brother and I were told to visit Granddad on the weekends, when things weren't going crazy, which they did as the days went on. I think my father emailed the school about the situation. I think it was Ms Papadopoulos he sent an email to. Also, Barbara, the school bus assistant, knew my father and mother.

So two people knew about the whole thing, which was fine with me. I didn't want a crowd of people asking, "How are you feeling? Are you OK? How's your granddad? How's his health?" That for me would have made everything worse. At school I tried to push everything to one side and focus on other things.

The days were ticking closer to prom and exams, but my mind was so focused on my granddad that the time flew past me. After morning registration one day, Ms Papadopoulos told me to wait because she wanted to speak with me. So I waited for most of the class to disappear, and I went up to Ms Papadopoulos's desk. She began, "Hello, Tom. How are you feeling?"

"I think I am all right."

"How're things going with the family? How's your granddad holding up?"

"I think I'm holding up. The family is, of course, worried and busy with Granddad. As far as I know at the moment, he's holding up. I have only seen him once or twice so far, but the last time he seemed all right to me."

Ms Papadopoulos was sitting behind her desk, looking at me with worried eyes. Maybe she thought I would break down in tears at that very moment. "Well, if you need anything, don't be scared to ask."

I said, "Thank you, Ms." After that I went off to carry out my timetable as usual.

A few days or weeks passed, and I got to see my granddad again in the hospital. To visit, we drove to the place and entered. The nurse or someone took us (me, my brother, and my parents) through some confusing corridors. Eventually, we arrived in the ward where my granddad's bed was. It was obvious that he was worse than the last time I had seen him.

When we reached his bedside, his eyes were closed. My father gently woke him up. Granddad's eyes opened and were a dull yellowish colour. He looked at me, maybe trying to recognise who I was. I think his left eye was a dark red, as if he had been in a fight. Which wasn't the case—I later found out that he had been confused and tried to wipe his eye, forgetting that there was a tube stuck through the top of his hand. As we tried to talk to him, often my father had to repeat the words more loudly for Granddad to hear.

We were at the hospital for a while before it was time to let him rest and recover. Then we went back to the car and drove home. There was an atmosphere of sadness in the car.

Naturally, I wasn't really paying much attention in school. I was super quiet in my classes and didn't say anything unless I was spoken to. As always, I kept to myself.

A few weeks later, my granddad passed away. When the news hit my ears, of course I was filled up with sadness like any other human being. However, I was shocked that I didn't bawl my eyes out for a week, which was what I was expecting. I just gave Father a hug for comfort and carried on with the day, playing games and doing schoolwork. My parents checked up on me in case I had a delayed reaction. I think both of them were also surprised at how well I took the news. There was something to be said for school: it gave me a way to carry on as normal, almost as if nothing had happened.

I can't say the same for the day of the funeral. I don't remember the date. My brother and I each wore a typical smart shirt, smart trousers, black tie, and black pair of pointy-toed shoes—a monkey suit, as I called it. I think it was an overcast afternoon as we got in the car and drove to my granddad's house. This confused me a bit because I expected we would go to a church, in common British tradition. I asked my father why we were going to Granddad's house, and he replied, "Because this is the way that Granddad wanted people to say their final farewells."

So we parked up and got out of the car. The first thing I noticed was that around the corner, there was a long, triangular car parked. Looking through the glass in the middle of the car boot, I saw a wooden box. I suddenly felt very uneasy.

We went through the front doors of the house and continued through to the extension. On the left was the staircase. The first room to the right was the living room. Straight ahead was the dining room; it usually held a big old table for six people. However, on this day, the room was almost stripped bare of everything familiar, replaced with a single, simple table in the middle of the room. I didn't understand why that table was there at first.

We went through the dining room into the kitchen. Pretty much all the family was there, as well as some people whom I didn't recognise. We exchanged greetings, music played, and I then found out what the table was for.

Granddad was a Hindu. I don't know if it's a Hindu tradition, but I watched an open casket funeral play out in front of me. Some men very slowly carried the casket in and placed it on top of the table in the dining room. Then the men left the house. A priest stood up and began his ritual by walking to the side of the coffin and lifting the lid.

There Granddad was, lying inside, looking like he was asleep. As soon as I saw him, I couldn't control myself any longer. All my emotions came to the surface, and I started to sob. Tears fell out like a waterfall. Father was beside me. I wasn't crying quietly; I was gasping for breath. I think I was so damn loud that my sobs dominated the house.

I wiped my eyes. People walked up to the body of my granddad, saying their final goodbyes up and personal, I guess. I was worried about what was going to happen. First to walk up were his brother and his sister. Then came my granddad's three sons and daughter. Then came the grandchildren, which meant that I had go up as well. I said that I did not want to get any closer, but Father said that I had to out of respect for Granddad.

I fought back slightly by holding on to my wheels, but my father pushed me and he was the stronger. There was no way I was winning that battle. Also there was a crowd of people, and I didn't want to create an unnecessary scene in front of the whole family.

So I ended up a few feet away from my granddad. My mother said that I should come closer. I quickly shook my head. I was already too close for my liking. I worked hard to hold back the tears while I was near. I don't know my reasoning; I think I didn't want my granddad to see me crying.

After a minute or so, it was time to let the next person say goodbye. I went back through the kitchen, to where I had been before we paid our respects. I thought that my granddad couldn't see me there. I couldn't hold it in any longer and cried hysterically again. My father then took me to the front room, where I sat down on Granddad's sofa and tried to calm myself. Father sat next to me the whole time.

Being in the front room did make things a little easier, I guess. Water was still pouring from my eyes, but my breathing was slowly becoming more controlled. However, many of my memories had been made in that front room. Over the years they had sadly faded, but one that I remembered most was that I started to walk independently in that room. I was ten.

Those thoughts helped me as a distraction from what was really happening. I sat in the front room for the rest of the funeral. Every now and then, different members of the family walked in to see if I was all right. First was my mother, who put her hand on my back. She said to my father, "You're missing the show."

My father replied, "Oh well."

My cousin came in and sat on the armrest of my seat. She put her hands on my shoulders and asked if I was all right. Lastly, my brother came in—I think the ritual had just finished—to seek comfort from Father. My brother probably needed him just as I did.

My parents, my brother, and I were all in the front room when my father spotted the casket being carried away. He got my attention and said, "Look, Tom," pointing. I saw the men carry the wooden box on their shoulders before the window frame blocked my view.

"What do we do now, Dad?"

"Now we have to go to church."

I just wanted the day to end but managed to keep my thoughts to myself. They loaded me into the funeral car, ready for the long, slow drive to the church. It was a Church of England funeral, which did puzzle me a bit because Granddad was Hindu. At some point, my father got hold of one or two water bottles. He said, "Try to drink. It will help."

When the priest began his speech, I was surprised: the water did help me to control myself whenever I felt overwhelmed by his words. The wooden box was up high. As the priest spoke, dark red curtains opened up and the casket slowly moved down into a small room. The people began to walk out while this was happening. I wheeled to the priest and thanked him for the service. The curtains slowly closed.

That was the last time I saw my granddad.

Afterwards, my father took my brother and me to where Granddad was buried. There was a stone with words on it which I couldn't quite see because it was covered with flowers spelling out the word "Granddad". I can't remember what we did right after that. However, when we got back home, we tried to carry out our days as normal. That's what I did, anyway, and most of the time it worked.

Until it was time to go back to school.

After Granddad's Funeral

My return to school started off well. Everything seemed back to normal, in a weird way. About a week after the funeral, I was leaving registration at the start of the day, or maybe I had gone into my classroom at break. I don't remember. In some fashion, I saw Ms Papadopoulos, and she wanted to talk to me. "Hello, Tom. How are you feeling?"

"A bit sad, but that's normal. I think I'm holding up OK."

"How're things going with the family?"

"They're coping in different ways, I guess."

"Well if you need anyone to talk to or want a moment to grieve, just ask."

"Thank you; I'll remember that."

It didn't take long before the weight of what had happened kicked in, no longer than a week or two. Needless to say, I forgot Ms Papadopoulos's advice. I just wanted to be alone, to find a quiet place to compose myself.

I found a classroom which I was allowed to go into at lunchtime. It was empty, which was rare. Normally a small group of people would be in the room at any point in time during the lunch break. There were some chairs to the left of the door, and I transferred to the chair nearest to the lockers. *At last, a moment of peace and quiet*, I thought.

I sat back on the chair. I tried to rest my head on the lockers, but that wasn't going to happen. (I blame my big head for that.) In the end, I sat straight back on the chair, resting my head on the window behind me. It was not the most comfortable position, but it had to do.

I tried to relax my body and let my mind wander. It was short-lived because a mate of mine banged on the window where my head was, giving me a massive shock. My mind hadn't realised fully what to make of the situation and went into autopilot mode. "Go away!" I shouted. I was aware enough to know I was starting to make a scene.

"Hi, Tom! How you doing?"

"I said *go away*. I don't wanna talk to anyone!"

I was worried that some teacher would hear me and start asking questions. That was probably the last time I spoke to that mate. I was so far away from the reality that nothing really mattered to me. He went off down the corridor, and I attempted to go back to my happy place.

I got a solid ten minutes of time to myself, thinking of my granddad and of me taking my first steps at his house. Those ten minutes soon ended. Another person from my year entered the room clapping. The sudden noise made me jump and snapped me back to reality.

The person quickly said, "Sorry!" With a slight giggle, he added, "I didn't see you sitting there."

I slowly transferred into my chair, thinking, *Yeah, right. Of course you didn't see me. You liar!* Then I went off to look for a different place to hide away. Before I knew it, the bell had rung and it was time to get back to form class. So I didn't have proper time to wind down and compose myself. I think it is essential to have time and not rush the process.

Work Experience

The school made a big point about work experience. Basically, for two weeks we had to go to a workplace—most commonly an office job—to have a taste of what employment in the real world was like. I was fine with the idea because it was two weeks off from school, which made me more than happy.

The school gave us a list of job titles with tick boxes next to them. We had to tick the ones we liked the sound of and give the list back to the teacher. The teacher came back a few days later with a letter saying, "So-and-so are happy to take you under their wing for two weeks."

I'll spare you the details. After a few discussions about what was more suitable and more accessible for me with my wheelchair, I was sent to the Barnardo's office in Barkingside.

Before I could start "work", I had to attend an interview. As I waited for my interview, someone called me into a conference room—you know the type of room. It had a long table in the centre and about fifteen chairs around it for huge business meetings. The person who was interviewing me was a woman named Pam. After ten or so minutes of conversation, I passed muster and was brought on to work the next Monday. I was *very* happy to go somewhere that was not school!

The first day of work was an introduction to the staff and what their job roles were. I had a tour around each department; it was like an endless stream of people saying hello to me. I replied with a smile and a nod. Sometimes I talked for a brief moment. I thought everyone seemed friendly and they were actually talking to me normally.

After seeing most of the floor, we went back to Pam's base. She placed me on the computers which would be my station while I was there. I think there were four people at one table, and the team was made of two tables. So technically I was working alongside eight people for most of the time.

Soon after I had greeted everyone, someone told me that I had to meet up with the boss. It felt for a moment like the childish thing in school when a teacher says, "Tom, the head teacher would like to speak with you!" and the whole class goes crazy. Anyway, I got to the boss's office and waited until she was ready to see me. The door soon opened, and I had a chat with her about what was expected of me while I was at Barnardo's.

It wasn't that bad really. She let me know that if I misbehaved, she would tell the school and I would be sent back. I listened to the rules and the consequence of breaking those rules, and I thought, *The idea of sending me back to school is enough of a threat that I won't misbehave.* Afterwards, I was free to go back to my workstation, where I waited for anyone to give me something to do.

Soon I was given the task of counting the coins in one of those charity boxes you see people holding on the streets. Time was running short, so they only gave me a box with a small amount of change. Basically, the money that Barnardo's gets in those boxes is sent to the nearest office. There, some poor soul (me) counts the change. They make up a pound and put it into a plastic bag. That was my job. It wasn't long until my day was over and it was time to go home.

The next day, my father took me to a nearby cafe, which was on the opposite side of the road. He then dropped me at the office and set off to his own work. This established a pattern for my two weeks. Once I was in the building, someone would buzz me into the office. Usually it was Pam who would then take me to the office desk to get started.

My main duty was to deal with a box filled to the brim with coins, or sometimes the coins were scattered all over my desk—hundreds of coins, all mixed up, and it was my job to count them and put them into bags. At some point, I got tired of picking them up one by one; that took forever. So I came up with the idea of putting the gold, silver, and coppers in three neat stacks. I could sort out the denominations from there. Occasionally there was a gold coin, but not many. I tell you, it was all about the damn coppers.

Once I got them sorted, Pam told me that there was different work for me upstairs. So we went up the lift and into another office with a whole lot of different people. After the hellos and smiles, I met up with someone who had another job sorted out for me. He gave me a big folder and a huge pile of papers, like the piles that you sometimes see in cartoons. My task was to sort the papers into some sort of order—I forget what it was now. Anyway, I thought, *Why not do the same sort of system I used with the coins?* So there was me with a handful of papers, trying to get a system going. The people in the office would offer me a drink, and sometimes I took a drink and sometimes I didn't. I didn't want to make a mess everywhere.

Before too long, I would go back downstairs to finish up with the coins. Because I had already sorted the coins into relevant piles, it was a lot easier, and it didn't take me too long to finish. Before I knew it, it was time to go home.

A couple more days of counting money and I think the coppers would have kept me up at night. So many coppers! Sometimes my hands would pick up a copper smell because there were so many coppers. But I kept my head down and counted them over and over until they come up to a hundred. Then I put the hundred into a bag and counted another hundred. I got faster and faster at counting and putting them into bags. The co-workers around me noticed and were shocked.

I'm making it sound like the only thing I did while I was there was count coins or sort out papers. Well, mostly that's right! But I did other stuff too, like sending emails. It was a bit embarrassing with the emails because I had never made up an email before. Pam had to write up a step-by-step guide on how to create an email. The last thing I was told to do was to create a fundraising poster or booklet type of thing. My two weeks ran short, so I had to finish at school. I think I sent it in by email.

All joking aside, the short time that I spend at Barnardo's was the right experience at the right time for me after what I had been going through. I had a fun and unforgettable time with the whole crew. The cool thing was that near to the end of my time working there, it didn't seem like work at all. I still have nightmares of the smell of copper!

If by chance any of my colleagues from Barnardo's read this, I just want to say thank you and it was a pleasure to talk and work with you lot. I've still got the card that you gave me, after so many years have passed. No, I didn't forget it or lose it!

One of Many Awkward Moments

Before we move on to my GCSE experience, I must say a few words about an episode in my food tech lesson. I had chosen the subject only because I got to cook my dinner in school, then eat it when I got home. You see, with Father working for most of the week, mainly late hours, he didn't get home till past time for my brother and me to eat our dinner. So we had to deal with my mother's "cooking", which mainly consisted of microwave pizzas.

So I decided to join the food class. We learned about a healthy diet, the food pyramid, how many calories were in a McDonald's breakfast (a lot!), and how to cook certain foods within the hour we had in class: pizza, pasta, sausage rolls, pastry, and sometimes cakes and apple crumble.

It was not all about cooking and fun, though. Most of the course was just sitting behind a computer, working on a Word document or a PowerPoint slide. That was not fun.

I bring this up because it was quite near to GCSE exams. There was pressure on us from the teacher to put our heads down, finish, and hand the work in on time.

So one day we all went up to the classroom. Being wheelchair users, Sarah and I had to use one of the lifts—the most unpredictable lifts anyone was likely to go in. There was only room for one chair inside, and it was a very rough ride up or down. But we both made the trip up safely and wheeled to our parking spaces. We waited for our names to be called, whereupon the teacher would debrief us of what we had to do in this lesson. Mostly it was "Finish up your coursework!"

While we took turns retrieving our school laptops, I noticed that Sarah was on a lower desk, just to one side of the classroom. The teacher said to me, "Tom, you're going to the desk to do your work. Get a move on." And she pointed to the same desk that Sarah was at.

As the LSA moved my laptop over, I slowly crept towards the desk. trying to believe that this wasn't real. *I am going to be sitting right next to Sarah! Only a few inches away!*

I found myself with my knees tucked completely underneath the desk, where they barely had enough room to move. If something made me jump, my knees would be the first to know about it. I tried hard to forget who was to my right and to completely focus on the work I had to do.

It didn't go well.

I struggled to type complete sentences or do any worthwhile work. My heart was racing at a hundred miles per hour. I could feel the pounding in my chest as if my heart were ready to blast out at any moment. I could only imagine the sweat that was pouring down my face and hands. I dared not take my blazer off!

When the teacher or the LSA come over to check on Sarah and me, Sarah seemed as calm as anything. On the other hand, when someone tried to talk to me, it was like I didn't know how to speak. What I did manage was a stuttering mess.

"How's the work going, Tom?"

"I-i-i-it's go-go-go-go-go-going gr-gr-gr-grea-grea-grea-great, th-th-thanks."

That wasn't all. My ear canals must have opened up. I could hear every sound ten times louder than it usually sounded. I jumped and jumped at every sound in the classroom. At one point my whole right arm was screaming in agony. The pain moved around to my back and left arm. So you can imagine what sort of mess I was in.

I can't even imagine how I must have looked in the eyes of Sarah. She was probably thinking, *What in the name of heaven is he doing to himself?*

That hour on that day seemed like a whole year to me. I wished desperately for the minutes to go faster. Finally the teacher told Sarah and I that we could leave early because the lift was so slow.

I can't remember if I rushed out of there as quickly as possible or waited for Sarah to go out of the classroom first. However, I knew that we were both upstairs, and one of us pushed the button that called the lift up. While we waited, I could feel the tension is the air. Every hair on my body must have been standing on end.

When the lift opened up, we looked at each other, no words spoken. We were both signalling that the other should take the first lift down. After a few nods, I held my ground and refuse to go on first. Nervous wreck that I was, I stayed true to my manners.

Sarah backed into the lift and put her brakes on. She pushed the button to go down. As the doors started closing, I looked at her. I don't know why—perhaps to make sure she got in all right? She looked back at me and gave me some sort of smile. It was automatic that I smiled back at her. The way I read her smile, she felt as awkward as I did.

Probably not one my best days, I tell you.

GCSEs: Before GCSEs

Before it was time for the big GCSE exams to start, I had grown so tired of the education system that I had stopped believing in the whole thing altogether. I even had a moan with a teacher right before the GCSEs about how I felt that school was standing in the way of my sporting career.

You see, this was after a team that I played on was in a competition and got third place. My team lost to the best team at the tournament—can't really complain about that. After the event, I wanted to take the path of a professional athlete. I didn't care if it was wheelchair basketball; I was willing to play any sport. Of course, any teacher would tell you that education was the best route to take for any career, including sport, but I didn't see it that way. I felt school was a colossal waste of my time.

So I said things to this teacher like "I don't believe that education is going to help me" and "I'm tired of waking up in the morning to go to school" and "I think a school has disabilities when it has so few facilities for people with disabilities".

That was the topic changer. I don't know why I said that, but the conversation became more about the school than about myself. I gave the teacher a big list of things that I thought were wrong about the school, and what I believed at the time should change to make life a bit easier for someone with disabilities. He was writing away in the notepad that he always carried with him, or at least that I never saw him without.

Needless to say, nothing was resolved this day. He just said, "Good luck with your exams", and we went off to our respective classes.

During GCSEs

So when it came to GCSEs at the end of the year, I had reached a point that I just didn't care about what grades I would get or what grades were needed for a particular job.

My school made students do some revision. Everyone from my year put their heads down, looking at papers and using coloured markers and all sorts of tricks to help them remember everything. I just sat there, looking down at my book to make it seem like I was doing something. I drew pictures with the coloured markers or daydreamed. My mind was going crazy with a billion thoughts trapped inside. Then I would get caught out by a teacher or an LSA and go back to staring at my book again.

Near the time of the exams, I purposely did some last-minute revision, which is the worst thing you can do according to some studies. I wanted to make out to the teachers that I was doing some form of revision at least.

When exam day finally came, a select few students were told to head over to a certain classroom. I was put into the far left of three rooms on the first day. It was the most humid room because the heat permeated it, and with no window, it got stuffy quickly.

The mindset I had for every one of my subjects except maths and English was to speed through it as fast as I could. Of course, I had to act like I was putting *some* effort in, so it wouldn't look like I was failing on purpose. I would never fail on purpose, of course.

For some of the exams, like history, I had forty minutes to spare, leaving me to just sit there until the time was over. My excuse was that in one year of history lessons, we had anywhere from six to ten different teachers. They all covered the same topics and the same pages of the history textbook, which got very annoying at the end. I knew that I wasn't going to learn anything in a system like that.

I think most other students went home as soon as they didn't have any more exams, but I had to go home on the bus, which meant waiting for the whole day of school to finish. One of the downsides of not being able to go home on your own.

However, in the end I was pleased with myself for maths and English. I wanted to at least get a pass in both of them. They were the results that nearly everyone looked towards unless you intended to do something specific. I got a C in both maths papers, a D in English language, and a C in English literature. To my eyes, those were passes. At least I got the bare bones for some form of life.

Prom May 2011

It was a few weeks after the GCSEs and all the pressure was gone. Everyone was buzzing about the year eleven prom. I didn't know what the hype was about; to me, prom just sounded like a huge party. Well, I did see it as something to celebrate the end of school. The worst part of prom, which I kept on seeing in every kind of media, was students asking if you were going to bring a date, and if so who would it be?

I do not know if you can call it luck, but luckily no one was interested if I was going to take anyone. I wasn't going to go, because what was the point? I hated parties with huge groups of people. The music was always too loud to start a conversation, and I just got shoved aside. I was one of those people who stood in the corner, talking to myself with a drink in my hand. Might as well put on a funny hat on as well.

With all that said, I decided to go ahead and go to the prom! I signed up and got my ticket from the school. I bought a sharp 'man suit', though I was not sure about the tie. I hated those things.

I got dropped off at the school gates, and I rolled up my sleeves just long enough to get inside. I went up and down roughly five speed ramps, then up the long slope into the main entrance of the school. I was the first to get inside, and they were still finishing up in the hall. I could hear them and see the movement of shadows through the glass on the door.

That was not the first thing I saw when I came in; the first thing was that someone had decorated the main entrance to be more welcoming for the prom. A bright red carpet was rolled out from the first step all the way to the main hall. There was a welcome board by the first door. However, the most notable change was a photo booth set-up. It had tall professional lights, a huge blue screen for background, and a tripod with a DSLR camera and a single chair to the side. The photographer must have been inside the hall, getting a drink or something.

I tried to give my entry ticket to someone, but they told me to hold it until the main hall was ready and people were allowed to enter. So I placed it back into my pocket and parked myself near the seating area, looking out a window. There wasn't much to see, just the fields to the left and some art that A-level students must have done.

It didn't take long for more people to arrive. Some of them waited at the benches with me. When the doors were officially opened, I waited in line to show my ticket to whoever was at the door. Then I was finally inside the main hall, and I didn't recognise it for a split second.

The stage at the front still had a microphone stand front and centre, a couple of chairs, and posters that read "Prom 2011" and showed pictures of individual students in their classes.

What caught my eye almost immediately were the banners looping down from left to right along the ceiling, all with the same sort of text.

The main part of the hall was completely empty, no chair in sight. I guessed this was the dance floor, where most of the madness was going to happen. Some chairs were against the side walls. Looking to my right, I noticed that there was a food table full of all sorts of party food. My first thought was that not much would be eaten, because I heard that after the prom finished, students were known to take a long limo to London for an after-party of sorts.

I had no plans to go to London; it was a big leap for me to go to school after hours. I wasn't going to spend even more time with my peers in London. That's what I told myself anyway. I was actually thinking that I wished I had a group of people whom I trusted to take me, instead of having to run back home while the night was still young.

"Thomas!" someone shouted over the music which had just started. More and more people were coming in. The shout snapped me back to the real world. I saw Ms Papadopoulos behind a table, filling up the remaining glasses that covered it. I wasn't sure what type of drink it was, but it was bubbly. "Tom, do you want a drink before the other students get their hands on them?" she asked me.

I raised my hand to indicate no. She somehow caught it and gave me a nod back to let me know that she understood me.

I kept waiting for something to happen, but it was too early. I went out of the hall to the main entrance and sat there instead to watch other students enter the school. I may have looked like a creep by doing this, but I didn't care. I noticed that the photographer was back and sitting in his chair, likewise waiting. It wasn't long before a group of friends went up to him and asked to be photographed, then another group, then a pair, and his services turned out to be very popular for the rest of the evening.

I couldn't help thinking how great it would have been if Sarah and I were up there, holding each other while having our picture taken. That would have made my prom moment for sure. Sadly, that was never going to happen, not in a billion years. The thought did make me smile for a second; then I started to feel sad. To snap myself out of it, I entered the main hall again, away from the photo booth.

Pretty much most people had turned up by then, and the night started to get a bit crazy. There was loud music and people dancing. Other people were walking outside, probably to get some fresh air. The hall was getting a bit stuffy because of all the people moving about at once. Yes, the hall often held more than one year's worth of students at a time, but on those occasions they were mostly sitting still.

At the halfway point of the prom, Mr Roberts got up on the stage and announced the prom king and queen, the best-dressed female, and the best-dressed male. I'm not sure if they did the best couple or not. Everyone was pretty quiet as the names were called. There was a rumble of claps and laughter after each announcement. I tried to capture some of the events with the mini video camera I had brought with me. But as I filmed, I missed the best bits. One of these was a teacher singing (I must admit, seeing your teacher sing is kinda funny). The prom king also leaped from the stage and got carried above the crowd.

I was too short to even lift the camera that high, and when I did lift it, I couldn't see if I was aiming at the stage or what I was filming. After a few attempts, I knew that I was never going to get the best film angle from where I was, which was at the back of the hall. I could have moved to the front of the crowd to get a better viewpoint, but that would have required fighting through the great mass of people. There was a high risk of hitting the ankles of every female who was in the middle dancing (of course, males too, but I didn't care about hitting them).

Needless to say, I stayed at the back, put my video camera in my pocket, and parked myself to the left side, far away from the food table. I stayed on the sidelines for most of the remainder of the evening. I was tired and had a massive headache, because I normally couldn't stand when the music was blasted out loud enough that I couldn't think.

However, I started to feel that my chest was pounding to the beat of the music, *boom boom boom*. At first this scared me, and I couldn't understand why—probably because it was unfamiliar. I tried taking deep breaths to make it go away, and to my surprise, it did. Then I was so damn tired that I yawned and placed my elbows on my knees. I rested my head on my palms, centring my mind with thoughts.

Suddenly I felt something on my shoulder. I raised my head to find Ms Papadopoulos standing next to me with her hand on my shoulder. "YOU ALL RIGHT, TOM?" she shouted over the music.

I took a deep breath and straightened my back. "YEAH!"

She took the seat to my right and leaned close to my ear. "WHAT ARE YOU DOING OVER HERE? WOULDN'T YOU PREFER TO UP WITH THE CROWD?"

I shook my head. "NO, I'M GOOD HERE!"

"ARE YOU ENJOYING THE EVENING?"

"YES!"

Soon after, someone from my year came up and asked Ms Papadopoulos for something. I couldn't hear what. I was miles away in my own little world. Ms Papadopoulos stood up, placed a hand on my shoulder again, and shouted into my ear, "I HAVE TO GO. I'M NEEDED SOMEWHERE. WHY DON'T YOU TRY OUT SOME OF THE FOOD? I'LL CATCH YOU LATER!"

"OK, I—"

But she didn't hear me as she walked off. It didn't really matter, I thought. She was helping out with the prom. She was bound to be busy.

So there I was, again on my own, watching my peers dancing, eating, or chatting. Don't feel sorry for me; I'd known what I was getting myself into when I bought my ticket. I sat on that spot for a good while, just watching the world go by, lost in my thoughts. I must have been there for twenty-odd minutes before I decided to move. People were starting to notice that I was sitting on my own, looking like a weirdo. So I moved randomly, this way or that way or maybe this way … I must have looked like a right fool.

I finally decided to head to the food table for the first time that evening. I puzzled over what I was going to have; there were too many options. I made my mind up on some tiny sausage rolls, picked one up, put it straight into my mouth, and then went for another. I was hungry.

As I chewed on the first, I felt something on my shoulder. It was like a slight breeze of cold air running down my spine.

"THOMAS."

Had I heard my name?

"THOMAS!"

OK, that time I definitely heard my name.

I turned around to see who it was, and I couldn't believe my eyes. There Sarah stood, only a few feet away, intentionally looking at me and speaking to me. It was only my name, but even that was more than I was expecting.

I met those deep brown eyes of hers, and she said, "Tom, your dad is waiting for you outside."

I could only just make out that something was outside due to the deafening music. But I didn't want to miss a word of what Sarah was saying, so I held my hand to my ear to signal that I couldn't quite hear.

She tried again: "YOUR DAD IS JUST OUTSIDE OF THE GATES, WAITING FOR YOU!" She waved her hand to tell me to walk with her. I followed, thinking she would stop at the front entrance. But I was wrong. She was taking me outside.

As we went through the corridor, I was so nervous that my hands were shaking. I tried to say, "Sorry, I cou-couldn't … h-hear you i-in there." At last I finished a complete sentence, but almost at once the butterfly feeling, tight knot in my stomach, and sweat from my hands and forehead hit me at the same time. All I could do was hope that she wouldn't notice. I simply hadn't expected that she would talk to me at all, much less walk by my side to the outside. Perhaps it was an overreaction. She was only taking me to my dad so I could go home. It wasn't *that* unusual. Maybe my head was working twice as hard because it was bored after three or four hours spent mostly alone.

We went through the automatic doors and down the long ramp. I tried to let gravity take my wheels, so I didn't have to use any energy with my arms. That would generally have been easy, but tonight I was next to Sarah, who was inches from me to my left. My arms and ribs suddenly seized up and made my whole body shake. My hands instinctively gripped my wheels, bringing me to a halt. This threw my torso forwards while I was fighting to keep straight. I felt super embarrassed and struggled to hide the pain in my shoulders and back. A little sound escaped me.

"Are you alright?" Sarah asked.

"Yes, I'm—" now holding my right shoulder, "—alright, nothing new really." Before I had a chance to look at her, my chair shifted to the right, so I quickly straightened it and continued down the ramp. I was ashamed of my little scream of pain and thought, *Could this not have happened anytime but tonight?*

Up and down, up and down my chair went with no further trouble for my body. We went down the drive, heading to the school gates. I don't remember if it was ten or eleven o'clock; it was an evening with a clear night sky and a few stars visible above us. I tried to look at her without her noticing.

I had not really seen her before this moment. She looked so beautiful with her hair upheld by a single band. It split her hair into two groups with curly ends, one on each side of her shoulders. She had a pair of cream-coloured earrings, with a necklace and a bracelet on her left wrist to match. I think she had a small, black, over-the-shoulder bag.

As for her prom dress—how do I begin? Well, it was mostly black, covering the tops of her shoulders and finishing at knee length. I especially noticed the lower half of the dress. It had a large design of a white, wave-like pattern going around and a single black spot at the highest point of the wave.

We were halfway to the gate when Sarah stopped. I realised this, put the brakes on, and turned my chair round to face her. I was very nervous. My head was coming up with all sorts of different outcomes, good and bad. When she spoke, it felt like time stopped.

"Thomas," she said, "you look good tonight. I would like to be friends again."

I said, "Yes. I very much miss that."

"So can we try and get past what happened?"

Sarah waited for me to reply. All of the sudden I had a rush of guilt that punched my gut. I remembered the disgusting things I had texted her, being a controlling creep about what she could wear and rude about her hair length. When I met her eyes and tried to reply, I struggled to get any words out. It was as if something got hold of my voice box and stopped me from speaking words.

"I-I-I wou—" I paused to clear my throat. "I would like that."

Come on! You can say something better than that! my mind shouted.

But it turned out that I couldn't. I just sat there and had one last look at Sarah, thinking, *This feels like the last time Sarah and I are going to walk and talk with each other.*

With a smile, Sarah said, "Come on. Your dad is outside. Don't make him wait."

All I could do was give her a nod of the head, because again I had a knot in my throat. Then she turned around and walked back to resume her time at the prom.

Come on, man! What you doing? You can't just leave it like this. "I would like that"? What sort of answer was that!

I wished my head would stop giving me all these thoughts. But my head was right. It was a stupid way to finish the night. As I watched Sarah walk away, I tried desperately to shout out something like, 'I'm sorry!" and possibly explain myself. How I had been afraid that my future would be dependent on others. Even an action as simple as going out to a restaurant meant I needed some sort of care. It wouldn't have been fair of me to ask her to ... Well. I didn't shout.

As she reached the bottom of the ramp into the building, I said to myself, *Nope, you had your chance, buddy, and you blew it!*

I moved towards the front gate, still very mad at myself for missing the opportunity to tell Sarah everything. I don't know what happened as I went up and down the speed ramps. I just couldn't go over them with ease like I usually did. It took so much energy. After the first one, my body was messing around, meaning my shoulders played up, which puzzled me. When I went over to the second and third, my back and ribs kicked me with sharp spasms that almost made me fall out of my chair.

What the heck was going on with me? My head gave me a sharp pain on the left side at the back. I just sat there for a moment, thinking everything was activating. Then I brushed it off and looked through the gates. There was no sign of my father anywhere! There was someone who kind of looked like my father—same build, same hair, and similar glasses.

That doesn't make any sense! I thought, looking back at the main entrance. *Sarah knows what my dad looks like!*

I took a brief moment to decide what I should do. I had two choices. The first was to go back inside, sit on the sidelines watching other people be happy, and chance another embarrassing encounter with Sarah. Maybe I would find her, take her arm, go somewhere I could talk in private, and explain everything in one huge moment. *Oh, go on then! Make the massive move of your life which would change everything! What have you got to lose?*

"No!" I said firmly and tried to shake it off.

The other option was to ring up my father and tell him I was ready to go home. Yes, that seemed like the best option, to go home and finish prom night.

Coward, taking the easy way out.

I took my phone out and rang my father. The whole time I waited for him, I couldn't stop thinking, *Should I go back to Sarah and explain everything in a big crying mess of "I'm sorry!"? I should at least go back and say thanks to the teachers for an enjoyable evening.*

Before I had come to a decision, my father arrived, and we drove back home.

"How was the prom, Tom?" he asked.

"It was all right," I said as I yawned, ready to get some sleep.

But I didn't get much sleep that night. My mind was racing with different thoughts jammed into my head, trying to break free. I couldn't settle. I think at one point I threw the covers off the bed in frustration and cried myself to sleep—but not loudly enough for my family to hear me.

Prom night is one of two regrets in my life so far. The first one, of course, is how I was not able to handle my romantic relationship with Sarah. The second is how I messed up my chance at friendship too. In neither case had I been able to say how I really felt.

These regrets I have carried with me until this day, and they don't seem to get any easier through the years.

8

Year Twelve 2010–2011

I do not know why, but I ended up in another year of school. Yes, I stayed on. I was so not looking forward to days of turning up, putting on my happy face on the school bus, and only talking to a handful of teachers and LSAs. I would go from class to class, learning things that I never actually used, and go home to sleep the day off—only to wake the next day and do the same. Sounds fun, right? Oh and the best bit! I would get more opportunities to make myself look like a complete fool every time I was around Sarah. Needless to say, I wasn't pleased to go back for one last year at school.

One of the first trips that the school arranged for the new year twelve students was to the local ice skating place in Romford. I wanted to find out more about the trip, so I spoke to one of the teachers who had announced it. I wanted to find out if I was allowed to stay at home rather than sit out the trip by staying in school. I don't know what I was thinking. The trip was on a Friday, so naturally the teacher said, "There is no choice. Either go on the trip or stay in school and catch up with your work."

The last thing I wanted was to be in school and carry on with my lessons as normal. So I was stuck going on the ice skating trip. Instead of jumping to a conclusion about this trip, I tried to keep my head clear and hopeful. That was the only thought in my mind as I sat at the back of the coach, pretty much by myself, my body gently moving from left to right when the coach turned the corners. My attitude was that the school had come up with this idea with the thought of people with disabilities in mind, as it was the "best" school for people with disabilities.

How was it? Well I can't remember a whole lot about the trip, which is not a good sign.

The only memory that I have is of sitting on the benches in the stands. Someone must have helped me up there, of course. And that's it! That was my experience at an ice skating place with the year twelve group.

I wasn't the only one sitting there. In total there were four people with disabilities in our year group, Sarah, me, and two others. We were all sitting on benches or walking around endlessly. In Sarah's case, she was sitting in her chair, near the fence that went around the ice, watching the people skating. Out of all of us, I thought that she had the best chance of putting on skating shoes and joining in.

Thoughts came and went in my mind. I would have loved to find a way to ice skate with Sarah. I quickly moved on from that thought before I started tearing up. I wished the school had come up with something to get students with a disability *involved* in an activity we could participate in. Maybe the skating place could have a wheelchair modified to go on the ice? Surely that wasn't too crazy? How hard would it be to combine two skis and a seat? Look up sled hockey.

As for propelling the sled, some form of stick to push would work for some students with disability. Or how about having an abled student or two push the disabled one? Unless they're heartless. I can see the possibility of students with disabilities bonding with fellow students in such an activity. Because to my knowledge, the purpose of such trips was to get everyone socialising with each other and forming new friendships.

I went into the school year with the intention of taking only two subjects, BTEC science and BTEC business. Evaluation of these subjects was coursework-based, meaning no exam at the end of the year. That was good news for me because I was terrible at taking exams.

The way the (BTEC) Business and Technology Education Council system worked was that you took any number of courses you wanted, and there were only three possible grades: fail, pass, and merit. (There may have been another one I can't remember.) A fail was a grade F, a pass was a grade C, and a merit was a grade B. If you wanted to get a B at the end of the year, you had to get a merit on all assessments. So if you get one fail and all the other assessments were merits, you failed the course. That's how I remember the system, anyway.

When I got my brand-new timetable, I was very pleased with just the two subjects. I had two or sometimes three lessons a day. At first, this was really good. Then, halfway through the year, the school changed my timetable, so more of my free lesson times were taken up by "private studies". This meant I was required to go to the private studies classroom or the school library, which sucked.

I got a pass somewhere which broke my merit streak. No matter what grade I got in the remaining assessments, I would end up with a pass or grade C. I could have gone back to improve that piece of work, but I was happy with the grade. Thereafter, I aimed to do just enough work to get a pass and no more. It made sense to me.

Some teachers didn't seem to mind. My business teacher got the idea and would only help me enough to achieve a pass. For other teachers, this attitude of mine became an issue. I'm not sure why. My only thought was that was what they were there for—to encourage us to achieve more within ourselves. I stood my ground and refused to spend more time on trying to achieve. I tried many times to explain to the LSAs and the librarian how the system worked and how I was planning to work it.

In the end, I just did my own thing. It almost got me in trouble with the librarian. I had caught up with everything the teacher asked me to do, and I didn't know what to do next. So I ended up doing nothing, which was very dull. If I had a chat with anyone, the librarian shouted at me: "You're making too much noise! Now get to work or I'll report you!" I tried to explain that I had no work to do, but she refused to listen to me. A couple times she kicked me out of the library. Fun times!

My feeling of loneliness was higher than ever before. Sure, there were one or two people I talked to, trying to keep hold of my sanity. I wished then that I could have some sort of time-travelling machine. I could jump forward to when I would finish school, so I could get on with my life and start fresh—a clean sheet or a new beginning, you might say. Or I could jump backwards into the past, when I would have a second chance at redeeming myself and fixing my mistakes. I could at least have another go at explaining myself to the one I loved about my actions, about my gut feeling regarding future of dependence on others, about— There I go again. Sorry.

There were many reasons why year twelve was an extremely difficult time for me. One of many was that I ate lunch, by myself most of the time, in the sixth-form common room. And every time I looked at the entrance, it seemed I found Sarah coming through the doors. I would experience a sudden rush of guilt through every part of my body, and also the need to escape. I still felt angry at myself for what I hadn't said after prom—how I had not fought hard enough to recover any hope of friendship between us, which was now unquestionably lost forever. There I go again! Sorry!

Apart from guilty feelings and regrets, there was something else happening. I was surprised at myself when I noticed it about halfway through the year. Amid the too little work to be done and too much private studies time, I was also having meetings with the school's careers adviser. I had met with her before about work experience and CV writing and interview practices—anything related to getting a job. This year, something about all that just clicked in my head. I realised that the adviser, the school, and my parents for that matter were all quietly saying to me that the *only* job I was likely to get was an office job.

No one said it to me directly. It took me a long time to fully understand what was going on, but the idea started in year twelve. I'm not sure if I straight-up confronted the adviser or my parents about the message they were sending me.

I must say that telling a person with low self-esteem that an office job is the *only* way to get money is not great advice. You can do anything—sport, music, theatre. If you have a natural gift for something, go for it. Practise, practise, and practise some more. Don't let anyone tell you anything else!

As the year went on, it was clear to me that they didn't really know what to do with me. I say this because the career adviser took one or two of my free periods to bring me into a classroom with other students with disabilities or low grades. We did activities that did nothing to develop any useful skills. As an example, she set up a touch-typing programme which

I had no choice but to do. If I refused to do the task, I got into trouble. Another activity was to play stupid games on the whiteboard. It was just meaningless stuff. They didn't know what to do with me.

Social Groups

This was when I realised that I always ended up in the same group of people, whom I called "low-grade" students. They were students who didn't do so well, and it showed in their work or exams. They needed some extra help.

Seeing how I acted in year ten, I can't exactly blame others for placing me in this group. However, in years eleven and twelve, I tried my best to get out of that group. But when I participated in class, I often was made fun of, and then I'd shut down and keep to myself. I had begun to notice that tendency in year eight, with my experience with the drums. It got worse in years ten, eleven, and twelve.

The clearest example of this happened in year ten. I was put in a group with two low-grade, "too cool for school" boys, and we were asked a question: What does the body do when a person gets nervous?

I don't know why a teacher would ask such a question. I came up with one answer, saying, "You get jumpy." It seemed a smart answer.

One of the other boys said, "No, that's just you," The third just laughed at this "joke", which shut me down completely. I didn't want to join in any group activities from that day onwards. I got told off for it sometimes, but, as happened too many times, I didn't care in the end.

I felt lost hanging out with these low-grade students. Some of them must have made me look smart. Sometimes they came to me for advice, such as how to talk to a girl. Girls were an alien race to some of them. I was the last person to talk about how to ask a girl out, but they thought that I was the master of the subject. This was amusing at times but also frustrated me.

One day I was in the library, finishing up some work, and some boys came in to talk to me. I was as friendly as I could be. Then I tried having a conversation with a girl from year thirteen, who was sitting at one of the desks. I left the group that I was "with", who were busy with something stupid to amuse themselves.

I went up to the girl, leaned my arms on a chair next to her for comfort, and started a typical conversation. You know the routine. "Hi. How are you? What you doing? What subject is that?" And so on. Nothing too interesting. But this was the first proper conversation I'd had with one person outside of the low-grade group since speaking with Sarah. I was quite pleased with how I was handling this conversation.

But the moment was short-lived.

In the middle of the sentence, I was interrupted by "Hey! Hey! *Hey!*" Just the sound of their voices was enough for me. I closed my eyes in disbelief and put my head down between my arms. "Look what we got here!" they shouted.

I thought, *Please just leave me alone to talk to this person in peace!*

"Thomas is trying to chat someone up. Hey!"

I wanted to scream very loudly at that moment. Then I remembered that I was in a library filled with other students, so I told myself over and over that I couldn't scream. Instead, I took a deep breath in and slowly breathed out. This was always my method to calm myself down. I raised my head, only to see the group of boys looking at me with their stupid faces. "Awww, Tom, you're blushing."

I ignored that comment. I was having a normal conversation, and that was all. I turned to the girl and said, "I'm so, so sorry about this."

"Don't worry about it," she said calmly, as if she understood the situation. That helped me a lot.

I tried to move away, outside of the library and out of reach of the boys who had ruined my conversation. This didn't happen. They buzzed around me like bees, making a joke of what they had seen. I understood this was typical behaviour in a school environment. But still, it could be damaging.

Everything that happened at this school was slowly transforming me into a lone fighter. I was only able to trust in myself, but I was too scared to take any necessary action. That was how I felt, anyway.

Last Days of School

Apart from all that, I was still talking to Ms Papadopoulos, giving her updates on my school life and how my basketball was going. One time she was on lookout duty. I walked past her, and she was talking to a pair of students. She stopped me and said, "Tom, how's it going?" She turned to the other two people and said, "This is Tom. He's a legend!"

I sat there with a smile, but inside my head, I thought, *Legend? What have I done to deserve being considered a legend?* I thought back on my last couple of years, wondering what I had accomplished. In the end, I couldn't think of anything that stood out, just memories of me being a rude, grumpy teenager.

Then Ms Papadopoulos asked if I'd heard anything from the head teacher these last two years. Actually, I *had* emailed the head, and she'd called me in for a meeting. I don't remember how it went because I was so nervous, but I know I did have a chance to explain how I felt about students with disabilities having nothing to do. Basically, I said that there weren't many activities or clubs that disabled students could go to.

That was the main part of the meeting. I focused hard to pull myself together and say the right words and not mess the whole thing up! After a few ups and downs, the head teacher had heard my points and made up her mind about what the school could bring to the table. She came up with the idea of making a small corner of the tennis court available for disabled students.

I'm not going to lie; I was disappointed by this. I tried to push her buttons a bit and said, "Is that your only idea? Have you got any other ideas?"

She said, "I'll have to go and think about other ideas," and added, "Thank you for bringing this to my attention." That was how the meeting ended. I waited and waited. Days became weeks, weeks became months ... you get where I'm going.

The meeting happened near to the end of the year, and this year was my last year of school. It seemed to be another moment of not having been strong enough to stand up and say the right thing. A feeling of disappointment overflowed me, and I went to see Ms Papadopoulos. She listened to my story and said, "Oh, sorry, Tom, school is almost finished. Sorry that you didn't finish your little protest." And I'd finished school with no idea of how my "little protest" went. It thought it had probably gone up in smoke because I felt no one really cared or listened to me.

I said my final goodbyes to Ms Papadopoulos and thanked her for helping me throughout my last three years of school. I also went to the PE department to say goodbye and thank-you for the opportunities I'd had with sports days and award ceremonies and pretty much everything sporting-related. I said goodbye to other teachers walking by too.

On my last day of school, I went into my form class, which was a science classroom, and I found everyone together. I was confused by what was happening. People were standing or sitting around one of the desks, and it was full up with a basketball written on in black ink. The class had all signed it. There was a tin of chocolates too.

A girl stood up and said, "Thomas, we all know this is your last day of school. You have been a great asset to the class, with you cheerful, hard-working attitude …"

I can't remember the whole speech. It did, however, bring a tear to my eye, I am a sucker for saying goodbyes, and before I could do so, the class was moving around, eating chocolate, and chit-chatting.

After that, I had a free period. I went to the common room to see what group of people would accept me. I told them it was my last day. They said, "Well, good luck." The bell went off again, and it was time to get onto the school bus for the last time!

This was the hardest goodbye for me, saying farewells to the driver, Barbara, and the helper, Nile. (I think that was how he spelled his name. I just remember it sounded like the river Nile.) They had been driving me from school to home and back for almost my whole five years of school. All in all, it was a great way to end my time at school.

Outside my house, both my parents were waiting. Father had his camera with him. Barbara pushed me to the ramp, and all three of us had a picture taken. After that picture, Nile lowered me onto the pavement. I said goodbye to Nile and thanked him for loading me up on the bus again and again. Barbara ran to the doors of the bus and gave me a big hug and a kiss on the cheek. My parents said goodbye as well. Then Barbara and Nile hopped back into the bus and gave one last wave.

That was the last of the goodbyes. I had officially finished my high school career.

2011 Personal Letter, Saying Goodbye

Start 5 July 2017
Finish 16 July 2017

Dear Sarah,

One of the surprise experiences that I had while writing this book was how much I could remember about you and the times that we had together. During our time at school, I tried to find a way to explain myself. However, when the time came to hand it over to you in person, I couldn't find the courage to do so. That's been haunting me ever since.

The time that we spent together was the most precious time of my life. And when it all ended, that was the first time that I was genuinely heartbroken. For some reason, I couldn't let go until I found a way to express my feelings.

So here it goes.

As you might know, I was going through a fair number of challenges during our early school years. We all were. For myself, I was struggling a lot with bullying, like the episode in drums class in year eight. That was such a devastating experience that, honestly, I was in a very dark place.

The only thought that kept me from giving up was the thought of seeing you next. Your personality just shines. I can't help but smile whenever we are together. I even thought about choosing drama because you showed me opportunities that I didn't know existed, like the day you took me to see your drama tutor, Mrs Potter. Each of you had such positive attitudes towards life. You showed me the possibilities beyond my wheelchair, instead of letting the chair control me. I wish now that I could have said this in person—how much you meant to me and what a positive influence you had on my life.

Then came the most significant change in my life: going to the hospital in year nine. I had to spend a good number of weeks in the hospital, and I was going through a lot of pain. When you came to see me, you supported me. It gave me the strength to carry me through that pain, so I could go home and see you again.

Home also meant the care of my parents. Don't get the wrong idea; I am grateful for their support. However, my parents were always with me. I didn't have room to breathe. Remember on my birthday, when we went to Pizza Hut? They drove us and stayed with us the whole time, which must have felt as awkward for you as it did for me.

Long story short, the overprotective nature of my parents set off warning bells for me. While I was resting at home, I came up with a theory that this was what my life was going to be like. I was unable to look after myself.

With that idea growing in my mind, I realised that I was thinking of myself when I should have tried to be there for you. That was selfish of me.

Nothing spoke to me more than Valentine's Day, when you made a handcrafted gift. That was the most beautiful "pressy" that anyone has given me. It had me in tears of joy. And how did I return the gesture? With a simple text, because I was too embarrassed to tell my parents to buy something on my behalf and post it for me. I can't imagine how frustrating that was for you.

I should have shared my concerns with you, and with your positive outlook on life, *perhaps* things could have been different between us.

It would have been good to know your family a bit more. They had a great approach towards disability that would have helped me understand. All I wanted was to make them feel proud and have confidence in me. It saddens me that I couldn't be that person.

There are no words to describe how selfish I was near the end. I should have just spoken to you as you were—my best friend, whom I had loved very much.

All I wanted was to be supportive and for you to be happy. I wanted to be as much of a positive influence in your life as you were in mine.

Sincerely,
Thomas G. Kandiah

9

2011 After School

Firstly, I want to talk about what happened a week after I left high school. I was given a chance to go to a disability independence boarding school. Or that's how I thought of it—I'm not sure what it's really called.

I don't know how to explain this place because I had only one or two lines to go by. From my understanding, this was where a disabled person like myself could go to experience what an independent lifestyle felt like. The staff watched you do some tests, like putting socks on, putting shoes on, tying up shoelaces, cutting up lunch or dinner, brushing teeth, getting shopping, and everything to do with the kitchen—all the tasks involved in independent living. Then they would come up with ideas and gadgets to help you with the staff you found difficult.

One day I was sitting in my room when Father came in and gave me this tiny description of what it was about. Now, I am a shy person when it comes to big decisions like this one. I never learned how to weigh up the options and choose the one that best fit me. So when Father dropped this 500-tonne weight on my head, I didn't know what to say. At the age of 17, I had to choose the best option for me.

The benefits would be that I would get a chance to be independent. I would enter an unknown environment and learn the skills necessary to start living my life on my own. I supposed I could stay with my family in survival mode, hoping to be taught those skills in future. The other possibility was that I would be with my family for the rest of my life. When my parents became too old and couldn't support me, I would be stuck with no knowledge of how the world worked or how to look after myself. I would have live somewhere that others could look after me instead.

Needless to say, I couldn't think this all through on the spot. I just froze, and no sentence came out that made any sense. What made it worse was that I thought Father was trying to scare me with the fact that it was a boarding school. He said I would be away from home for a long time, completely on my own, with no help from him or Mother. I would have to feed, wash, and shop by myself. On and on and on he went.

My final decision was that I would pass on this opportunity and go to college instead.

Thinking back on this moment, this was a turning point that almost determined my life for the years to come—in a negative way! I rejected the perfect opportunity to learn to live on my own and be my own person.

On a positive note, you can read about how my life went after this moment. Enjoy!

Secondly, I want to talk about my experience with abseiling at Lambourne End. It happened in May, so I was still finishing school, but the experience was outside of school and one of my personal favourites.

When I joined up with the youth club, True Colours, meeting new people and making friends was great. However, the best bit was an outdoor activity centre called Lambourne End. I can say it was the most fun I'd had in a long time. After some negative times during the last years of school, it was good to do something I got some enjoyment out of.

I did many activities during my times at Lambourne end: rope course, caving, archery, fencing, rock climbing, campfire, a midnight walk in Hainault Forest), and on-site visiting of farm animals. All this in three visits!

As you can imagine, I tried every activity they'd set up each time I went. I put 100% effort into whatever task they placed in front of me. I tried every rope course, including the one over a freezing-cold pond. I explored the smallest cave tunnel they had, even though I had to slide down the tunnel with a team of instructors to help me.

In the archery session, the instructors placed balloons on a target. The goal was to pop every balloon. I popped five of six balloons! Not bad, I may say.

The last of the highlights was the midnight walk through Hainault Forest. A head torch was the only guide. I didn't do my job properly and didn't see a huge tree stump in front. My carer walked me into it, and I flew out of my chair. I was all right, and it was completely my fault and loads of fun. After that walk, we had a huge campfire with stories and singing.

The reason I tell you all this is because one of the highlights was having the opportunity to try out wheelchair abseiling. It was apparently the very first programme of its kind in the local area, and they wanted me to be one of two people to be the first to use it. The second person happened to be a friend from school, Isaac. I can't speak on Isaac's behalf, but I personally liked the idea of being first. Someone told me that the event would be written up in the *Redbridge Recorder* newspaper, which meant I had to go with the opportunity. A chance to be in the newspaper? I couldn't refuse that.

So on 9 May, both my parents took me to the centre. My father pushed me from the car park to the main compound, where a small number of people were gathered with drinks and snacks, mainly staff members. I think that this early, we were waiting for Isaac. My father had his camera with him and was taking photos everywhere he went.

After a few minutes of waiting, we saw a taxi parking, and we knew that it had to be Isaac. The boot opened and the ramp was put down; then a wheelchair backed out of the taxi. There was a bit more waiting so Isaac could get settled down with a drink. A few more minutes, and we started to walk towards the site to see what Isaac and I had gotten ourselves into.

We came across a huge hill. A hut with a small roof was on top. A rope blocked off the entrance to a ramp. Past the rope, the ramp led to a dirt path. From the bottom of the hill, it didn't seem that intimidating.

We carried on up to the hut, where we got geared up. The gear was mainly a helmet and a harness. The helmet was tricky, trying to find one big enough for my enormous head. I had to settle with the next to the largest one, which still didn't fit. It was the best they could offer me. The harness was easy to find in the right size but very tricky to put on. My father had to ask for help from a staff member to make sure the harness was in the right place. When Isaac and I were sorted, it was time to have our first encounter at the top of the ramp.

Isaac was the brave soul who went first. He was able to stay in his wheelchair because it was the right type to use for abseiling. The brakes were on, so he didn't go backwards. All connected, he was slowly pushed backwards over the edge and began his descent. I can't imagine how he must have felt that first time. His chair was, at points, swaying from side to side while his mate tried to position it to continue going downwards. I was nervous for him just watching from the top of the ramp—not too close to the edge obviously.

When Isaac was about halfway down, the staff members began preparing me for my descent. I had already transferred into another chair that was more suitable for abseiling. My own chair was a different design from the standard wheelchair, and they didn't want to damage it.

I was already facing away from the ramp, away from the edge, so I was happy enough. My father was back at the start of the ramp, and my mother was near me.

When the staff members were satisfied that Isaac was safely down, they retracted the rope and put it in place again. Then they slowly backed me towards the edge of the ramp. I got more nervous the closer I got to the edge. I couldn't help myself. I made a witty comment to an older member of staff. Luckily he took it lightly and made a jokey comment back, which made his helper on the ropes and me laugh. I always had a great relationship with everyone working at the centre.

And having a few laughs was good for distracting me from what was about to happen! Imagine how many emotions I was going through while waiting to go down there. So many!

When they connected me to the system, a woman explained to me how it all worked. I'll try to keep it simple, mostly because I've forgotten most of the details. The wheelchair and I were connected to the pulley system with a number of ropes and knots. There were two separate sets of ropes, one for myself and one for the wheelchair. The reason for this was that if something did happen, the wheelchair would crash to the bottom, while I would be swinging on my set of ropes. I would likely smash into the wooden boards of the ramp, which was one of the reasons for the helmet.

Meanwhile, a man was just finishing the set-up. He grabbed a black rope which had been pulled up from the bottom of the ramp. He passed it on to the woman to loop through the pulley system. As I was looking at the pulley system, I notice two ropes. The man gave me one rope and told me, "This rope here is how you would control the descent of the chair. Just feed it through slowly, and the chair will go down."

"What happens if I let go?"

"Then the chair will freely run down the ramp. The woman is at the other end of the rope which is connected to you, so you will be swinging in mid-air."

I was a little worried that the whole experience depended on me holding one rope to control the descent. He must have read my expression, because his next comment was, "So in other words, whatever you do, control this one rope and don't let go. Otherwise you will be sending me downhill with you!"

My first thought was, *The perfect opportunity, I think!*

Again he must have read my mind, because I saw the woman laughing and the man said,

"Don't you even think about it!" Which got us all laughing. So all set and ready to go!

As soon as the wheelchair moved backwards, I became nervous, not knowing how near to the edge I was but knowing that I was getting closer. I got nervous going backwards on a flat surface at the best of times—not knowing what's behind me is kind of scary to me. I also hate going near edges of any kind, like the top of the stairs or the kerb of the pavement, because one false move and I'm going to have an unfriendly meeting with the ground.

So going backwards and over the edge of a 30 to 40-degree drop, you can imagine how shaky I was. But the chair kept on going backwards and finally went over the edge. I think this had to be the worst part. As soon as the back wheels met the tipping point of the ramp, I leaned forward as much as possible. My feet were up in front of me, reaching for the sky.

I held the black rope tight with both hands; I wouldn't have dared do anything else at that point. I just wanted to get moving, to be honest. Some encouraging words came from the pair who were with me, and shouting from my friends behind me.

Once I was over the edge, it got a little easier. I was still holding on to the rope for dear life and leaning forward, mind you. Every time I fed the black rope through, it got easier, and the angle of the chair straightened more. Nevertheless, I was a bit shaky, which was why I had someone going down with me. At one point my chair swung to the right a bit, and he had to tell me to stop. That let him pull the chair to the left, and then I could continue.

My arms felt such relief once I had my wheels on the ground. It had been a fun experience, but it was tiring to hold on for that length of time. Still, I had the desire to go up the hill again and have another go. They said it was best to save my strength for when I had to demonstrate abseiling in front of a crowd—including the mayor of Redbridge himself!

So we got into our own chairs and headed back to the main compound of the centre to have food and drinks and to gather our strength.

Eventually we returned to the equipment hut and geared up in the same helmet and harness that we used before. We had a chance to meet up with the mayor then, and had a short chat. He asked how we felt, and I said, "A bit nervous!" We also had the press. They wanted to gather us up for a photo for the *Redbridge Recorder*. So we all bundled up and smiled for the camera. After that, it was time to show off this new wheelchair abseiling course!

I went through the abseiling one more time. It was everything I described earlier, with the added feature of a crowd which included the mayor of Redbridge and his family. The only difference was that I was thinking, *If I mess up on this one, the mayor will see, and it won't look good for the centre. So don't mess up!*

Again, Isaac went first and cleared it. I went after him and pretty much cleared it in one smooth descent. All the way, people were cheering. Once I made it down safely, there was another huge cheer.

Then we had another little chat with the mayor and shook his hand. Most of us went back to the main compound to rest up, and some of us said our goodbyes and went home. I said my thanks and my goodbyes to every member of staff I met at the time.

Once I was home, I made sure my father kept an eye on the *Redbridge Recorder*, looking for that photo with the mayor. After a week or two, my father called me into the kitchen and there I was, in an actual newspaper with a headline.

I'd made it to the newspaper! I was *so* happy! It became my favourite conversation for at least two weeks, just explaining to others how the whole experience was.

That was in June. Then life got a bit busy for me.

Sometimes after school, my parents told me that they had won a court case on my behalf. Apparently my granddad had put in a lot of time helping out. They were happy about this whole thing, and I was a bit confused about what was going to happen next. Until that point, I had believed that I would be dependent on my parents for the rest of my life.

Carers

Soon after we won the money, Father suggested that maybe we (mainly meaning me) should try having carers to take me out of the house a bit more. I went along with the idea of having carers to see what would happen.

My father and I went to see the manager of the youth club that I was going to at the time, Amy. We settled on the idea of trying out some of the people who worked for her caring agency. She kindly gave me four people to test with, since neither Father nor I knew much about having carers.

The first few times, I didn't know what to do. We would go to the park or to a restaurant, and I would try to get used to talking to other people, mostly the carers themselves.

On 4 August, I didn't know what to do, so my carer came up with the idea of going around to his house to help him bake a cake. I don't know his reason for baking the cake, but I went along with it anyway. Honestly, it wasn't the most entertaining experience that I've ever had. Part of the reason was that I was being told what to do, rather than having the full experience of putting the ingredients together. Which was nothing new and remains a common experience for me to this day. Most people don't believe that I am capable.

After that day, the carer announced on Facebook that he was having a pool party with everyone in the youth group on 11 August. He specified that everyone must go into the pool at some point. I didn't know what to make of going into the pool. Ever since my operation, I had stayed away from any large areas of water, from swimming pools to the sea. I only felt safe around water if my father was with me, because I knew that he wouldn't let anything happen to me.

After I talked to Father, I wanted to go to the party—but I didn't want to go into the pool. Nevertheless, I brought some trunks with me just in case.

At the beginning, the party was all right. People moved in and out of the house, getting food and drinks. When I eventually went outside, I found a table tennis table. As soon as it was free, I sneaked up to it, pushing as hard as I could through the grass, and waited for someone else to go on the opposite side. After a few minutes, someone got the hint and went to the opposite end with a paddle in hand.

At the same time, people were getting thrown into the pool by the host of the party. I admit it was quite funny hearing people begging not to be thrown in and screaming when they were picked up. At one point, a victim lay down, making it difficult for one person to lift him up to the height of the above-ground pool. So the host asked for help. Other people grabbed the victim's hands while the host grabbed his feet and started swinging back and forth. When they gathered enough momentum, the host counted "Three … Two … One!" And everyone let go at the peak of the swing, leaving the victim to fly high and straight into the pool of icy water.

It wasn't long until the host ran out of people to throw into the pool. He nagged me to change into my swimming trunks so I could go in. Despite my protests, I somehow lost the battle, and my mate showed me to the toilets where I could get changed. After some difficulty, I managed to change and went back outside.

Soon the host picked me up over his shoulders, leaving me dangling like a sack of potatoes, and slowly walked to the pool. Someone offered to jump in to make sure that I was stable enough in the pool. I thought the host would throw me in as he did the others, but instead, he lowered me in slowly. That water was *freezing*! I thought of getting out straight away, but then changed my mind. After so much trouble getting myself into the pool, I didn't have to get out immediately. It sounds crazy, I know, but I didn't want to be disrespectful.

So there I was, standing at the edge of the pool, so *cold*! Then two more people were thrown in. One of them decided to splash me with water, which I couldn't do anything about. I tried to splash her back, but with my left hand holding on for dear life, I couldn't do much with my right.

Don't get me wrong; it was great fun. However, after spending ten minutes in the pool, I had had enough. No one else was willing to join me, and I had gotten bored. I shouted for the two people who had helped me in. The host stood at the edge, ready to lift me up, while the other one jumped back into the pool to give me a boost from my legs. With teamwork, they got me up and out.

I leaned against the side of the pool, waiting for the man in the pool to get out, so they could both help me to walk. I wanted to get back into my wheelchair. But someone got a towel and placed it on the grass where the others were hanging out, so I was directed there instead. I ended up lying down, letting the warm heat from the sun dry me.

To begin with, this was all right, but then something started happening. Firstly, my lower back became painful. Then both of my shoulders went into spasms that felt like electric shocks. I tried my best to hide my discomfort from others. However, my legs started contracting and tightening up, pulling in towards to my body. It was almost as if my body was trying to roll up into a ball. When I tried to push my legs outwards, the pain was almost too much to bear. So for the next half an hour or so, I lay like a turtle on its back, rolling back and forth in an attempt to get on my hands and knees. I was like this for almost the rest of the party. It was a bit of a weird conversation starter.

"Um, Tom, why are your legs in the air like that?"

"Tom, are you in any sort of pain?"

When I returned home, I tried to get answers from Father, but he didn't know why my muscle had acted the way that they did. The closest answer I was given was that my body reacted sensitively to freezing cold temperatures, and not in a normal way. I haven't come up with a better answer than that over the years.

Needless to say, after that day, I haven't come too close to any pool of water either.

A short time after the pool party, I hired my cousin to join my pool of carers. All my cousins were suddenly interested in hanging out with me, and on 14 August, I arranged to stay at my nan's house. She wanted to take me to Colchester Zoo, which I thought would be fun. I hadn't been there in a while. Last time I had gone, my brother and I watched my nan drink Diet Coke to see the funny face that she made (she hates Diet Coke).

So I was at Nan's house, waiting for my cousin to come round and pick me up. She came round, had a cup of tea with Nan, and drove me to Colchester Zoo. We did the normal stuff that everyone does at zoos: go around to see as many animals as possible, then eat, then go to the gift shop, and then go home. The day went all right. However, when it got to about one or two o'clock, it turned into the hottest day of the summer. I was in my manual chair, so my cousin had to push me all the way around the zoo.

Colchester Zoo is built on hill after hill after hill, and these are not your everyday ramps on the streets either. I'm talking about 40-degree angles. These were *nasty* hills. The hills were a pain for my cousin to push me up. She had to take frequent breaks at the midpoint of most of them. But what goes up must go down, and that was the part I hated the most! Going downhill in a wheelchair makes my hairs stand up. It didn't help that my cousin didn't have full control of the chair. I was grabbing the wheels myself, acting like brakes on a bike.

It was no surprise that when we got to the African part of the zoo, my cousin said that the heat was getting too much for her, and she wanted to head back to my nan's house. There was nothing I could do except agree, after seeing only half of what the zoo had to offer.

* ✳ ✴ ✳ *

A few weeks into experimenting with carers, I remembered that on one of the holidays I'd had, a set of pool tables had been lined up somewhere. My brother and I tried every morning and lunchtime to get a table. If one was available, we would be on it as quickly as we could. Father would give us a few £1 coins and tell us roughly how to play. We picked up the basics very quickly. After £5 or £10, Father would say, "That's our limit," and we would get off to find something else to entertain ourselves.

I bring this up because one of the carers said to me that there was an arcade in Romford that had a couple of pool tables, and maybe I should check it out. I bet they're regretting saying that now. After that, near enough every time I had a carer with me, I would say that I was going to the pool tables. I filled my pocket with £1 coins and stayed for hours. Forget going outside and getting fresh air—who needs that?

Even with my friend who was my first carer, I just took him to the pool table rather than what we'd used to do, which was take in different cultural experiences: theatres, comedy shows, and that kind of thing. I do kinda feel bad because I had so much fun going to see ...

I don't even remember what we used to do before the Romford pool tables. Sorry, Gavin!

And I still feel bad about accidentally poking him in the eye with a pool cue. He was helping me chalk up, and I lined up my next shot. I moved too quickly, not looking at where Gavin was, and I accidentally stabbed him in the eye. Gavin, sorry, and I hope your eye is better now after five years!

Shoulder Injury

At about the same time, I entered a boot camp for wheelchair basketball. It had only been a year and a bit since my team came in third in competition, and I was still happy going to my club every Friday. I was putting in as much effort as my body could manage.

One week, my coach at the time was teaching us how to shoot towards the net. I didn't have enough strength behind me to lift the ball further than 2 to 5 feet, or very close to the net. To compensate for this, I had developed a method of using one arm—my left and only good arm—to do most of the work. It took me months of practising before I made my first basket. When I achieved that, I was very pleased with myself, and my coach was happy.

However, I was not an attacking player on the team, and I rarely took any chances of shooting, whether in a practice game or a proper game. One of the memories that always comes up in my mind is that in a practice game on the club court, I found myself right underneath the opposition net, and I had the ball in hand. I didn't know what to do exactly. I had been taught to look for a teammate who could shoot, and pass the ball to that person. For some reason, though, I forgot that. I looked straight up from under the net, ball in my left hand, did a fancy movement of some kind, and flicked the ball into the air. I must have put some right spin on it, because when the ball hit the left side of the rim, it went over to the right side. It somehow stayed inside of the rim, spinning clockwise over and over till it decided to drop through the net.

When I turned around, trying to get through the crowd of players so I could speed back on defence, I heard from my mate and assistant coach, Tyler, "What a great shot!" After the training was over and we were getting a drink, Tyler, Roy, Paul, Jaspal, and other players all stopped by to tell me what a great shot I'd made.

So why am I telling you this? Well, my shooting form was based on power from my left arm. I swung my ball joint around and used everything I had to power the basketball into the air. My shoulder was under constant strain and pressure, week after week.

Despite this, I got an eight-foot hoop in the driveway and shot for about an hour every day. My practice time was bit unreliable; it depended upon when my parents had had enough and wanted to go back inside. That was fine with me in a way, because when you rely on others sometimes things get in the way and they can't help you.

I completely understand that situation. Try not to get the wrong idea. I know what I must sound like. I'm not so blind as to not see that possibility. However, over time my frustration grew. I felt like I wasn't putting in enough hours to have any chance of competing at a high level.

With this slight increase in my shooting practice, I was ignoring my head coach's advice that I might cause injury. I started to experience a little pain in my left shoulder. I didn't pay any attention and carried on with my normal Friday night training.

After months of ignoring the pain, it slowly got worse, to the point that I couldn't sleep on my left side. That was a nuisance because it was my favourite side to sleep on. The pain escalated until I had to see a specialist in wheelchair sports. We went to the GP first, and the best advice from them was to see a specialist. An MRI scan might be needed.

When we got home, we ate dinner. Father wanted me to understand exactly what I was getting myself into if I got an MRI. The only person he knew who had had an MRI was Granddad. Father told me what Granddad had felt about his experience—mainly that he felt claustrophobic in the tube, and the best thing he had found for it was to close his eyes and think of something pleasant. As soon as Father said that, I was thinking, *I have a good idea what I will be thinking about while I have the scan.*

When I went to see he specialist, I think on 19 August, I was with Father, but I decided to speak for myself. Normally I let Father speak because he knew most of the fancy words that doctors liked to throw around.

I had to have the MRI before the specialist saw me. We sat in the waiting room for some time. When I at last got in the room, Father helped me onto the bench and swung my legs round to lie flat. Father must have told them about me jumping, because just before the scan started, one of the techs came by to sort out blocks to hold my shoulder in place. It was a bit uncomfortable, but somehow I managed to stay still. I was hoping that the whole experience would be over and done with as quickly as possible.

After the blocks were in place, another person came into sight with a pair of headphones for me. She said they should muffle the sound of the scan. She put them on my head and went back behind a projection screen, where two people controlled the machine. My father stood there too. All were wearing blue "armour" for protection.

The first thing that came to my mind as the bench started moving towards the scanner was that I had entered some sort of science fiction movie! I closed my eyes, keeping in mind what Granddad had said to Father.

At first, it went OK. I couldn't hear the scanner at all, except a slight hum. After the first pass, the technicians spoke to me through speakers. It startled me a bit, just enough for my headphones to fall off my head, even though they had warned me about the speaking before the scan began. They realised that I had moved and asked if I was all right. For some reason, I couldn't find the words to tell them that my headphones had fallen off. I just gave them the normal response, "I'm all right."

"Do you want to continue?" a male voice asked.

"Yes, I'm fine to continue."

That was a little bit of a lie on my part. For the next hour (it seemed longer inside that tube), I listened to the scanner move to each position with a massive *click*! I tried hard to keep my eyes shut. The temptation was always there to take a sneak peek and see what was happening. I tried as well to muffle my ears so I didn't recognise the industrial sound of the scanner. I tried with all my power just to think of the only thing that made me happy: beautiful brown hair, deep brown eyes … However, whenever I came close to seeing a full picture in my mind, it was interrupted by the heavy *click*, and I lost the picture altogether.

The scan seemed to take forever. I was jumping pretty much every other time they tried to take a picture, so the image was never clear enough. Finally, they got a picture good enough for the doctor to see what was wrong. They told me it wasn't perfect, but it would do—unless I wanted to come back another day to see if they could get a better picture. I immediately shook my head: "NO WAY."

Father, Mother, and I sat in the waiting room for half an hour before the doctor called us in. After a brief introduction, he sat down to his computer, clicking away. Then he turned his screen so we could see what he was doing. He went through folder after folder, trying to find my scan. Eventually he found it. I must say it was a bit cool seeing an image of my shoulder after seeing X-rays of my legs over and over.

For a few moments, he taught us what he saw in the scan. He pointed at the top of my shoulder and said, "There's a mass of white colour." Father and I were not quite sure what we were looking at. The doctor explained that the white was my nerves, which for some reason were not getting the information needed to repair themselves. He said there were two options for me: an operation that *might* work—no guarantees!—or a needle jab of a long-lasting painkiller which would help the nerves heal.

Everyone looked to me to decide. I felt the pressure. Was it worth having an operation on my only good arm, the arm that I relied on for my basic functions? I was confused about what to do. Father said on my behalf that we might need a bit of time to make a decision. At the same moment, I said (or tried to say), "The operation feels like too much of a risk."

"OK, so shall we try the needle jab, then?" the doctor said.

My father replied, "Can you give us any details about what Tom has to do for this treatment?"

"Well, if we do proceed, firstly we would use an ultrasound to see inside the left shoulder. Then we would use the image on the screen to guide the needle where it should be and gently move it so the painkiller is at the right spot, where it will work at its full potential. This treatment is very common among professionals and Olympic athletes. After that, you go home and rest the shoulder for six to eight weeks. During this time, I would advise Tom not to do any high-energy activities, like basketball. After the eight weeks have passed, he would come back to see me for an evaluation and to talk about any other options."

The first thing that I thought of was me not playing snooker for two months.

The doctor continued, "Are there any questions?"

Without thinking, I just said the first thing that came into my mind: "So does that mean I can't do any pool or snooker? Because that's the new thing that I have got into now."

The doctor looked a bit puzzled. He started to think aloud about how high a snooker table would be for a person at wheelchair height. As he waved his hand around, he said, "Not really, because the table is how high?"

"Um, about this high." I showed roughly how high the table looked to me.

The doctor carried on. "So the table is at this height, putting the shoulder joint at a strange angle to start off with. Then you have to move it to move the snooker cue to hit the white ball, which may cause an additional strain …"

Basically, he told me that playing snooker may not be the best sport for me, and after the injection, he strongly recommended that I shouldn't be at the snooker table for those two months. I wanted to slap my head. *Why did I bring up snooker to the doctor?*

I understood what to do, and I was ready, so we went to the other side of the hospital to wait for this injection. After what seemed like a long time, I was finally let into the room. This time around, my mother went with me. She helped me onto the bench, which was a bit too high for me. She sat next to me, holding my right hand, because I felt unsteady. I was also holding the edge of the bench with my left hand for further support.

The doctor came in and checked that I understood what I was doing there. He double-checked himself about which shoulder to inject and where to begin with the needle. When he got the details right, he dragged out the ultrasound machine. He warned me that it would be cold, and he wasn't joking! I startled a bit, which caught him off guard. I explained that there was a high chance of me jumping if a loud noise or something that I was not expecting happened. He seemed to understand.

He showed me a small screen. I could see the inside my shoulder. Then he moved the scan around to find something on the very top of my shoulder. To me, it looked like a white spot. The doctor explained it was where the tendon was damaged. Having found the spot, he got the needle, put the liquid into it, and injected into my shoulder.

Honestly, the only thing in my head was, *Please, no one inside or outside make a noise, and I will be fine.* That's my mindset every time I have to face a needle. People ask me if I am afraid of needles. My answer is always the same: "No, I'm not afraid of needles. I'm more scared of any noises that might happen as the needle is in me."

When the needle pierced my skin, I closed my eyes and prayed that no noise would happen. When I opened my eyes, I saw my shoulder on the screen alongside the tube shape of the needle. I think the doctor slightly missed his mark because he was gently moving the needle into position. The feeling of a needle moving slightly is weird. I think what made it a bit freaky was I could see everything on the small computer screen. I tried to stay calm the whole time, which was difficult because the temptation to move was ever-growing.

After a few left and right wiggles, the doctor got to the spot that he was looking for. He then warned me that it might be a bit cold. It was good that he had listened to my earlier statement, which doesn't happen often.

With a countdown from three, he pushed down on the syringe. He wasn't kidding about it being cold! Once again I closed my eyes.

Once the painkiller was inside my shoulder, the doctor soon removed the syringe. As soon as my arm was free, I couldn't help but stretch out to loosen up. I made my back straight, arms and legs stretched out as far as I could reach. I felt so much better after that! The doctor got a cotton ball to clean up the blood coming from the tiny hole the needle had made, and patched it up.

After that, I was clear to go home. Luckily I had no carers on that day, so I could have a much-needed rest. I had the next day all to myself too, a Saturday. I spent most of my time wondering what to do if I couldn't go to the snooker hall. At this point, snooker had become my primary goal in life.

The doctor's words were clear in my mind: "During this time, I would advise Tom not to do any high-energy activities." The last time I was given advice, I had ignored it, and it had caused my left shoulder to be painful. I was going to listen to the doctor this time around.

This led me to a conversation with Father. "What do I do with the carers now?"

I think he said, "Just think of something else. You are paying them to take you out, so think of somewhere to go."

This was not helpful at all because I didn't have a clue. When the carer came round, I had nothing planned. Father and Mother didn't give me any ideas, so we sat at home playing video games. I think at the time I was playing Halo on the Xbox 360, and we did that for about eight hours. Keep in mind that I paid him.

I'm not sure how long this lasted. I think it was a week. Then I just couldn't face having carers play games all day long, entertaining them rather than using them for my benefit to do something productive in my confused, messed-up life.

This was the first of many times I felt that having carers sometimes got in the way of my personal life. I really needed to rest my shoulder to have the best possible chance to heal. However, because I had carers for most of the week, I was encouraged to return to the snooker hall. So my shoulder didn't have a chance to heal, and possibly was made even worse.

October

My left shoulder was becoming almost too much to bear, so my father looked for physio in the area. It was quite difficult because, once he explained to them that I had CP, they would automatically say, "No, I can't work with that type of disability" (or any kind of disability for that matter).

After some searching, my father found one. Funny enough, it was near my best friend's house, the R brothers' house. We went to see him and explained that I was having some problems with my left shoulder. He agreed to have a look. He tried heat pads, electric shock, and acupuncture.

A few months into treatment, he started trying to get me to walk. He focused first on my legs. Then he worked on my back, because sitting in a wheelchair took its toll. Trying out a new toy one day, he clamped my feet and ankles to a bar. He pushed a guard down so my feet couldn't move. Then he flipped me upside down! No, I'm not kidding. Here's the proof.

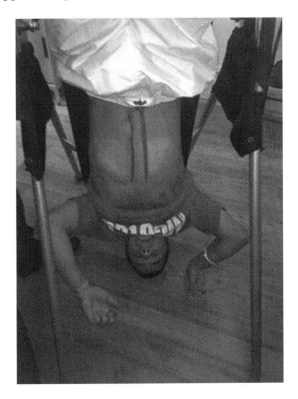

(9 October 2011)

Crazy, right? And you thought I was making this up!

After a few goes at this crazy machine, he removed the backplate. My ankles took 100 per cent of my weight, and I was left hanging around. (Ha-ha! Sorry!) It was a killer on my ankles. But as for my back, the feeling of it straightening out was very weird. At first, I had a sudden pain, but soon after that, I relaxed with relief.

I was in this position for thirty minutes. If I stayed relaxed, I was fine. However, when I had my spasms, it wasn't the best place to be. After spending that much time upside down, blood rushed to my head, making my face warm and red. Also, I lost feeling in my ankles sometimes, as there was little blood reaching that area.

When the thirty minutes were up, he would slowly flip me back to standing. Normally I felt light-headed and needed to rest. I felt many pins and needles as the blood reached my heels and toes. It took awhile for the numbness to go.

I had a few more of these sessions, and they helped a little. I was feeling excited because Father told me we were going on a Mediterranean cruise.

The Mediterranean Cruise

When we got to the airport, we had our bags scanned. Being in a chair, I couldn't walk through the gates, so the beeper went off. I was asked to step aside so they could check me. It didn't help that I had metal pins in my leg.

Then we were told to go to another area to get my chair wrapped up to go on the plane. We went there and explained that my chair had to protected. Before they could start wrapping my chair, we had to wait for a spare wheelchair, so I wouldn't have to walk too far. We waited and waited and waited … A small crowd started to build up, I assume for the same thing: to get a wheelchair. We all waited for half an hour. Finally I noticed someone pushing an empty wheelchair towards us.

The airport assistant looked at us and smiled, and I knew that this chair was for me. I didn't expect what happened next. An elderly couple was waiting as well. As the attendant approached me, the lady got up and said, "That's for us." Once Father realised what was going on, he told the person at the counter. She moved from behind her desk and caught up to the elderly couple. She explained that the wheelchair was supposed to be for us, and we had been waiting longer. It was no good. We had to wait for *another* wheelchair for a further fifteen minutes. By then I was feeling very fed up.

At last I transferred to the other chair. Father got a special bag for my wheels to go in. He disconnected my wheels from my chair and placed them in the bag. I think it had extra padding inside so the wheels would survive the journey, which they had to do because they were the only pair that I had. As for the seat of my chair, the airport had a unique machine, a huge shrink-wrapping machine, which spun my chair round and round in some sort of material, almost like the mummification of my wheelchair. After this, we went to the waiting area to meet up with the rest of the family.

Once the plane was ready for passengers, we all queued up and slowly began to board. When our turn came, I had to walk onto the plane. My father parked the airport wheelchair to one side, and I stood up with his help. He held both my hands and walked backwards at my pace. Our seats were almost to the very end of the aeroplane. After I was seated, I was fine. If you have been on a plane, then our flight was pretty much the same as yours: no unique story to tell there. Things were normal all the way to Italy.

Within a couple of hours, we had safely made it to the airport in Italy. We waited for the bridge that connected the terminal to the aeroplane. Then everyone grabbed their bags and walked down the aisle to the exit. Father and I waited for the majority of people to clear out before we started to move, so I wouldn't slow people down.

When the plane was near enough empty, it was time for us to start moving. It was the same manoeuvre as before. This time I tried to see past Father so I could tell him if he was going to hit anything. The process was a real team effort.

We walked to where they kept the passengers' wheelchairs, which was basically a tent. Father and I scanned them, looking for any signs of my chair in the crowded mess. It didn't take long before my father found my frame. At least that had made the journey. Shortly after finding the frame, we concluded that there was no sign of my wheels. My legs were getting tired from standing for too long, so I borrowed a chair before my legs gave way.

Father was still searching for my wheels. A man asked if I wanted to sit in my chair frame. Father tried to explain that the wheels for my chair were not there. The man was having trouble understanding us because his English wasn't very good. We in turn didn't speak Italian, so it was a very difficult situation.

Father thought that they might have put my wheels in the wrong place on the plane. We waited. Twenty minutes later, at last, we saw my wheels coming towards us. The sense of relief was unbelievable. Finally I could sit in my chair. It was much better sitting in my own wheelchair. We said thanks to the people, and they apologised for the inconvenience. Now we could join the rest of the family and get our bags from the baggage carousel.

We gathered ourselves and went to the cruise ship. Upon my first close-up of the ship, I couldn't believe how huge it was. There was a red-carpet entrance with a rope splitting the queue into two groups. Men and women stood in uniform on either side, checking tickets and allowing us in.

As we walked into the ship, we were mesmerised by how massive the inside was. After a first look at everything, I noticed something more important than anything else: the floor was flat. I know it's a strange thought, but one of the more common things I think about when going to an unfamiliar place is how flat the ground is. My shoulder was still screaming in pain, and areas decorated for comfort usually had thick, heavy carpet that was a nightmare to push on, even with healthy arms.

The passengers split up into groups, and each headed to their rooms. Father, Mother, my brother, and I all went to the lower level where our rooms were. Mine and my brother's was a disabled room, which was larger than usual. It had a bathroom large enough for my chair to do a 360-degree turn, two single beds, and a TV. I was a bit worried about the single bed because I tended to fidget in my sleep. I sleep in a four-foot bed if I can, and when that's not possible, I prefer to have a bed on the floor. Father and Mother's room was the next door down from us, so if anything did happen, at least it wasn't far to get help.

The first couple of days were all new and exciting. I stuck with my family (mostly my father) to learn the layout of the ship and what events were going on.

One evening there was a formal dinner. We had been warned about this in advance, which was why I had to pack a suit for the trip. I needed some help getting dressed that evening. I was fine with the trousers, shirt, and jacket. However, when it was time for the bow tie and formal shoes, I was in discomfort. The bow tie was pinching my neck somewhere, and the shoes were squeezing my feet so much that they really hurt. But there wasn't any alternative; I had to suffer this discomfort for the whole evening or sit in the room alone.

So now I was geared up for dinner!

The dining hall was huge, tables and chairs everywhere. Somewhere, there was a table for ten with name tags above the plates. Naturally, we changed the order of the names around on this first dinner night. When all of us had sat down, the staff members introduced themselves. After that, it was time to order food.

The food was so delicious and presented in such an artistic way that it was a shame to eat it at times. I was hungry, and I ate the whole thing with no questions. I wiped the plate clean. Our bellies full, we were feeling a bit jet-lagged—well, I was anyway. I went to my room, and my father helped me out of the monkey suit. It was such a relief for my toes when Father took the shoes off. If they could have talked, they would probably have screamed out, "Freedom!"

My brother and I couldn't sleep, so we watched a film. Then we crashed out for the night. I tried to find a position that I could be comfortable in for the whole night. It was not easy to do, take my word for it.

In the morning, my father woke us up, banging on the door and asking us to join the family for breakfast. We got dressed and went up the elevator to the floor with the food. It looked like everyone else had just woken up too.

We knew that we were stopped somewhere, and decided it must be Greece because that was our first scheduled stop. We sat outside in the sun and noticed that there were loads of people standing to look at something. My father and brother went over to check out what was going on; it was too tricky for me to go see for myself. It turned out they were just looking at ships going by and the shades of colour on the rock surfaces.

It was time to get food!

My family got up, leaving me to save the table. This was a technique that many people used while eating out with me. It was always a strange time for me, waiting for the family to come back. I didn't have my phone. It was in the safe. I looked down and messed around with my thumbs. The plus side was that it's always exciting to look up and see your plate of food heading towards you.

We talked about the food we'd been served last night and what we were thinking of doing while the ship was docked. My little cousin took a sudden interest in trying to push my wheelchair. She did this while I was eating. I grabbed my wheels to stop the chair from moving and waited for someone to tell her to leave me in peace. She was pretty strong for a 6-year-old.

Most of the evenings ended up with the family going to a bar area, which wasn't bad, but my brother and I were under eighteen, so we weren't allowed to have an alcoholic drink. We normally had a can of Diet Coke, which wasn't my idea of how a holiday should be. Often my brother and I would joke about how drunk our father was.

The day came when we got off the ship for the first time, which was exciting. When we walked off the ship, we were conveniently close to the taxi pick-up point. My father checked if he had enough euros to use in Greece, which he had. So we decided to take a taxi to the nearest shopping or food area.

We waited for a driver who was willing to take a family of four and had space in the back for my wheelchair. You'd be surprised how fussy some people are about anything disability-related, no matter where you are. About three drivers looked our way and saw the wheelchair, then quickly drove off. One driver stopped his car and asked where we were heading.

My father said, "A town, somewhere nearby."

The driver seemed to understand a little bit of English. He replied that there was such a place. He offered to take us for a little sightseeing trip. "How much would this detour cost me?" my father asked.

"Um, let's see, about 25 euros."

"At 25 euros?"

"Yes, 25."

"We can do that." My father seemed happy with the deal.

The driver opened the back. My father first pushed me into the car, then helped to get the wheelchair into the back. Everyone joined me in the taxi, and we started our little tour of Greece.

I looked out the window at Greece while half listening to the driver giving my father talks on all sorts of topics. It was very funny seeing my father trying to keep up with the driver's stories and join in on the conversation, which included some history lessons, mainly about the first building he wanted to show us. He told us that this huge arena was where the ancient Greeks had hosted the first Olympic games. We pulled up and parked on the other end of the street, so the family could take a look. I stayed in the car because it was easier that way.

After we saw this, the driver dropped us off at a market. We quickly got out, and Father told the driver to meet us in the same spot in an hour and a half. We watched the driver drive off, and we walked through the market street.

As we went, I immediately noticed that the paths were cobbled. This set off warning bells in my head because cobbles are a wheelchair nightmare. The front wheels are quite small and can easily get trapped, flinging me out of my chair like a slingshot. So while my father was pushing me, I kept my eyes down, looking for any gaps that could jam my wheels.

The market was very busy. I felt uncomfortable, as everybody seemed to be looking at me like they'd never seen a person in a wheelchair before. This was normal in my case; I have the same experience in any public environment that I put myself in.

In the rare moments that I could see what was on the market, I saw two T-shirts that I liked. They had cool designs on the front. One of them was a Spartan helmet design. Below was printed, "THIS IS SPARTA." The other had a design of a Spartan hoplite. I'm not sure what the rest of the family got while in Greece.

We found somewhere to eat, then headed to the opposite side of the market. We found a bench to sit on and waited for our taxi man to come back. Ten minutes later, he reappeared. The driver stopped at various places on the way back, and we took pictures.

After another short detour, we arrived at the taxi depot near the cruise ship. The driver parked his taxi, and we all grabbed our shopping and my wheelchair. Once we were out, we were watched my father talk to the driver.

"How much did that trip cost?" my father asked.

"That will be 80 euros, sir."

"Eighty!" There was shock on my father's face.

"Yes, sir."

"But you said it would cost 25. I'm not paying 80."

The driver stuck to 80 euros.

"Here's 60 euros. Take it or leave it, because I'm not paying 80 euros for that little trip."

Eventually, the driver took 60 euros. I think he knew he wouldn't get a penny more. With kind words and a handshake exchanged, my father pushed me while my brother and mother took the shopping. The events of the day were the key topic of conversation among the family for the rest of the evening.

The next morning, the ship announced that they were going to start moving to the second stop, which was Turkey. Loud horns sounded, and we moved away from Greece and onto open waters.

We had a lot of time on our hands, and it was time to explore what there was to do onboard. For most of the time I was with family members, which was fine, I guess. One time there was an ice-shaping event, and most of the family went to see it. They sculpted a huge block of ice into two seahorses within half an hour.

After they had finished, my brother and I went to play table tennis, which I really enjoy. It's my second favourite sport apart from basketball. I think it's because there's not much movement in table tennis, and I naturally have quick reflexes.

Hanging out with family could get a bit too much for me. My brother and I searched the ship for a while and found a small arcade area, which was good because I could spend time there alone.

Before long we were nearing the next stop, which was Turkey. As before, we discussed what we would like to do once we got off the ship. Seeing that this was Turkey, my brother and father talked about getting Turkish kebab and Turkish delight, the real deal.

The ship came to a stop and we walked off. This time we were within walking distance of the shopping area in town. We had only walked a short distance when we came across a very steep downhill, a thing I hate more than anything. As we reached the beginning of the descent, I grabbed my wheels with both hands, stopping the chair from moving any further. My father asked if everything was OK. I roughly explained that I would not go down this monster of a hill.

My father finally understood, and I tried to walk down the hill while someone else pushed the wheelchair. Father supported me step by step down the monster hill. It took some time, but I preferred safety over time any day. I had to take pit stops in the middle because my legs were telling me that they hadn't had to do this much work in a while. When we made it near to the bottom of the hill, I quickly jumped into my chair. My legs cried out in relief, happy to stop working so hard.

We came to a food area and sat down to try out a Turkish kebab. Then we went looking around the shops to see if there was anything worth picking up. At a sweet store, my brother immediately asked if we could buy Turkish delight.

After that, we headed back to the ship, which was fine until we came across that massive, evil hill. Sadly, this was the only way back. Going uphill in a wheelchair is not that bad for the person sitting. However, I can't imagine how much of a pain it is for the person who has to push me up. I'm not the lightest person out there.

We went slowly up the hill. I heard my father starting to breathe heavily. I asked if he was all right. Of course he said he was. I think my brother or my uncle helped him out after a while. After some sweat and tears, we made it to the top, and my father took over again, leading us to the ship for a well-deserved rest.

That was my experience in Turkey.

So what else did I see on the cruise ship?

There are *loads* of activities to do on a cruise ship, too many for me to write about. That said, I want to talk briefly about the gym.

I overheard my uncle talking to my father and brother, and we were all interested in checking the gym area out. So as a group, we went to see the gym. We had to walk through the swimming pool in the middle of the ship, which can be a bit embarrassing for a young man with his family when people in their swimsuits were everywhere I looked. For the most part, I stared at the floor until we were past the swimming pool.

Once we were inside the gym, we checked out the equipment they had. I wondered if they had anything safe for me to use. Sadly, the only equipment I could use were all to do with arm workouts, and with my injured shoulder, that wasn't wise. I watched my father and brother try out the equipment. My uncle talked to the gym instructor about classes. I sat and laughed at the funny moments of seeing my family work their butts off, while I had the perfect excuse of an injured shoulder. This was as entertaining as it got for my holiday experience.

On the third and final formal night, I dressed up in the monkey suit and evil pointy shoes. We four walked down the hall to join the rest of the family at the table we had used for all three nights. We sat down and looked at the menu, which had slightly changed from last time, and ordered our food. As we were finishing our main course, lights and music started playing, followed by special applause for the crew and restaurant staff. After a speech, we all grabbed our napkins and waved them above our heads. It seemed to be the ship's way of celebrating the last night.

I was still jumping out of my skin every time my little cousin tried to push my chair. Then she fell over on her back, yawning. I sat next to her father, and he found it funny, so I tried to play along and laugh with him.

My uncle and I were having a conversation about disabilities. I was trying to explain something to him, when I noticed my mother on the other side of the table. She was pointing at me and nudging her sister, saying what a surprise it was that I was speaking to my uncle for so long. I tried to find out what she meant, but she just shook it off. I was puzzled by the comment. It reminded e of other oddities in my mother's behaviour, which had first started way back in 2006. But I quickly stopped thinking about that when it was time for dessert.

Then we went to a bar area that we hadn't tried yet. The grown-ups were still drinking wine, beer, and vodka, while my brother and I were still drinking diet soft drinks. My father had the camera on him, and my family wanted to have photos done because it was our last formal night. We took turns posing in different pairs and groups. Here's me on my own.

Looking at this photo, I only wish that someone had fixed my left sleeve. It looks so off-putting. I spent the whole night looking like that!

We stayed up way into the night. I still had my little cousin chasing me to push my chair around the hallway. Then Father helped me onto a seat, which was more comfy, and my cousin immediately jumped into the chair and tried to wheel it away.

It didn't take long till she was tired. She sat between her father and myself. I thought that I still had the video of *The Lion King* on my phone, and it might be nice to see if she would like to watch. I checked with my uncle first, and he gave me a nod. So I opened up the film, turned down the noise so it wouldn't disturb anyone, and tapped her on the shoulder. She happily took my phone, As soon as she heard "Circle of Life", she was hooked, I looked at my uncle, and we both smiled.

However, it was short-lived experience for her. Just as she was getting to the end of the song, apparently it was time for her to go to bed. So I had to take the phone away, which she wasn't that happy with.

The next morning at breakfast, I heard a whisper among the family that one of the parents wasn't happy with me for showing her the film. That puzzled me. Why would anyone get upset about two cousins watching a Disney video together? I'd thought I was doing some good, but obviously not.

Looking back, I should have realised that in the unlikely event I had to get off the ship quickly, I was on the ground floor and the lifeboats were on the second floor. If the lifts were unavailable, how the hell was I to get up to the second floor? The only way for me to safely get off the ship would be to have my father or brother carry me up two flights of stairs and onto the lifeboats.

There had been talk of an evacuation at the beginning of the cruise, but they didn't mention how to get wheelchair users off the ship. This experience has made me think twice about cruising in the future.

Thus the end of my Mediterranean cruise.

Jumping ahead to 22 December, there was buzz about Barry Hearn dropping by the club to do a little promo, the kind when they take a short break from snooker after a couple of frames on TV. The owner of the club asked me if I wanted to meet the chairman of snooker himself.

To be fair, I had only been interested in the sport for a few months, so I was quite new to the history. When I asked my carer, "Who is Barry Hearn?" he thought I was joking at first. Then he explained that Barry Hearn and another professional, Steve Davis, had made snooker into the sport that it is today. After learning that, my first thought was, *Well, how can I refuse such an offer?* I had a chance to meet the big boss man himself!

When the day came, I went through my normal routine of three to four hours of practice on the snooker table. After practice was over, I packed up the snooker stuff, gathered the pool equipment, and went next door. During my third game, Barry Hearn and the owner of the club, Richard, came in. Luckily for me, I was taking a shot and potted the ball. Then I went up to Barry Hearn and shook his hand.

Our meeting was short, as he was busy. The conversation is very fuzzy in my head. Richard helped me out a bit, saying things like, "Tom has been coming in the club and playing snooker every day for three months, practising for long hours." Barry Hearn made a joke that he would see me on the main tour soon. I said, "I hope." Someone said something about a photo, so I set my phone up and quickly showed Richard what button to press. I managed to get a photo with the chairman of snooker!

Then he had to leave because he was running late. It was really cool that he spent a little of his time with me. I finished the frame, and while my carer was setting up for the next one, I went to the bar to buy a Diet Coke. That was my excuse to chat with Richard about what had just happened!

College (aged 17, 2011)

I want to talk about my time in college in one block rather than stretch it out through 2011 and 2012. The reason for this is because my overall experience with further education wasn't positive. That said, there's a story I want to share with you.

Near the end of school, our teachers and parents made a big deal about planning for what we'd do after finishing school. The main opinion they threw at us was college, college, and more college. "Because if you go there, you will have a better chance of getting a decent job further down the line." That was the number one reason they would repeat over and over.

At the time, I got into sports coaching, mainly for wheelchair basketball. The first step for that was to get a grade, then go to a coaching course, then go to a more targeted course for wheelchair basketball. The courses were followed by a coaching assessment, after which I would be ready to try out being a head coach. That was the path that I would have liked to have taken. I spent a few weeks checking out different colleges and what course I was going to take.

Also, my after-school hours with the carers seemed to be working out. I needed someone to take me to and help me with college. My father came up with a payment system for a carer which he was happy with, so that was sorted.

So how did it go?

Honestly, not that great.

The course met three days of the week, so that was a positive. Also, most of the teachers were all right to talk to. And ... that was about it.

It started out all right—a new environment, the introduction to the course, and the people who were teaching us. But then there were the students.

Now, I don't know why, but I had thought that if I was going to college, the people there would be a bit more mature. I soon realised that wasn't the case. I'd often heard about how common it was for first-year university students to goof off and then have a mountain of work to do in the second year. However, the people who were in the sports course with me were nuts! I described them as out-of-control zoo animals most of the time.

That was even before they knew about my jumpiness. As soon as they learned that I jumped at any noise, they took note, and at every opportunity, they made loud noises.

So I had been happy to leave school and get away from the negative feelings and the bullying, only to go to a different educational building with a different bunch of people and face a similar type of bullying behaviour again.

Something tells me that I am not meant to be in any educational system.

Apart from the bullying, the first half of the course was all right. The only memory I have is that the teacher tried to change up the sports for me, like changing the rules of basketball such that everyone had to touch the basketball before a shot could be taken. Another task was a workout track with all different types of exercises. The tutor came up with similar exercises that I could do from within the wheelchair.

Those ideas worked. Other ideas didn't work as well, such as one of the ball games, for which the whole class had to sit down on the floor. I appreciated the effort to make my experience better, but the whole class didn't have to suffer for it.

College Part 2 (aged 18, 2012)

As soon as the teasing began, I wanted to leave college very badly. I thought, *Nope, I'm not going through this again. If I do, I will go completely insane.*

I decided to say something to my father. I waited for an opportunity to say what I was truly thinking. When that chance came, I said stuff like, "I don't want to go any more. It is too much like school. I just want to stay with the one thing that I'd enjoy, which is to play snooker all day every day!" (I have a feeling I wrote something very like this already.)

Needless to say, Father's reaction to this wasn't happy at all. He repeated the reasons for staying in college. However he strangely focused on the idea of me playing snooker more than anything else. He was strongly against the idea. That threw me off a bit, because I thought the debate was about college. He also brought up another tack: "I don't want you to be stuck indoors all the time. It's unhealthy. I want you to go out and explore the outdoors." He concluded, "You need to stay and finish the course."

I did not like it one bit. To stay for a full year at college and be picked on most of the way wasn't going to happen.

Father and I went back and forth, almost shouting at each other. In the end, Father came up with a compromise: I would spend half of the year at college, and if I still felt the same about it, I would be allowed to drop out. I didn't have any strength to continue, and I knew that I probably wouldn't get a better deal. So I agreed to spend half the year at college.

Which was weird, because I was nearing the age of 18, which technically made me an adult. However, I was still going to my parents for solutions to my problems. If I wanted to leave college, I could have, because I was at the right age to make my own decisions. But I wasn't allowed to by my parents, whom I relied upon to make the hard decisions for me. That was probably why I didn't feel like an adult, but like a big child.

My father's words were "Think about it", but my mind was pretty much made up. Still, I honoured the bargain. Each week I attended college, I tried to look like I wanted to be there. This couldn't have been less true about the class that taught us how to prepare for a job. I was put in for group exercises. We were given a task that required all members of the group to take on certain roles. Needless to say, very few tasks were ever completed. We were moved on to creating posters or something. Then our focus suddenly switched to the steps we were required to follow if we chose to get a job. And that was why the problems start to arise.

I think it was nearing the end of the term when they asked us to start thinking about writing up a CV. If we had a CV already, we could improve that one. I did not have one because I had no use for one, given my primary dream of one day becoming a sports star. Coaching was my fallback option.

So on the day that we had to write the first draft of our CV, I felt I had little background of achievement that was worth putting down on paper. Yes, I had won a good number of medals and trophies in school, but I didn't feel that was relevant for a completely fake CV that most likely was going in the bin. I chose to stick with my basketball background. With that in mind, I had written down my achievements: wheelchair basketball club, third place in a wheelchair basketball competition, and a go at every disability sport that I could think of.

On top of my achievements, I had to describe myself in a positive manner. The terms I put down were these: I have CP (cerebral palsy), and I am a full-time manual wheelchair user. (I wish I had kept the copy of my first draft.) I felt that was a fair account.

With the first draft done, we had to print it and hand it to the teacher. Then we had to wait a week to get it back so we could make the changes.

A week later, we came back to class, and we were handed the first draft to look at. While the teacher was talking to other students, I skimmed my first draft to see what changes I had to make. I had to read it a second time to see if I was looking at it properly. What I saw on the second reading was that the teacher had edited with a red biro pen, crossing out all the disability terms and every use of the word "wheelchair". I couldn't believe what I was seeing. It took me a while to come back to reality.

When the teacher came around to me, I asked, "Why have you crossed out the wheelchair and disability words?"

She replied, "Because there's no need to label yourself. The person who is interviewing you will see for themselves. That way they can form their own judgement if you are the best fit for the job."

I didn't know what to think, honestly. Should I be angry and get into trouble? In the end, I was in such disbelief that I didn't know what to make of the situation. I was also a bit thrown back that my carer, who had heard all that with me because he was sitting next to me, didn't say anything. Presumably he had official training in working with all kinds of disabilities and had learned the proper terms to use when speaking to or about a person with disabilities.

Strangely, this incident didn't bother me as much as high school had. It still bothered me, mind you, but I didn't quite understand the effects of a lack of knowledge until I was faced with the situation in college. On that day, I should have spoken my mind despite the consequences, because I had a feeling that this was discrimination. But at that time, I didn't have the right words to express my feelings.

Anyway, I shamefully made the changes that were on the edited paper. I didn't feel right doing so, but to save any trouble, I did it anyway. At that moment, I knew I didn't belong in college.

At the end of the lesson, the teacher said that the next week, we would be practising a one-to-one job interview. Still frustrated with myself that I hadn't put my foot down earlier, I made my mind up that I wouldn't go to this job interview practice, especially because she had said that it was required to get a pass in the whole course. Knowledge that I would fail the course further strengthened my decision to leave when the half term came round.

Again, keep in mind that I was paying the carer with my own money.

On the day of the practice interview, I had to say something to my carer about what I was going to do. Once I did, he wasn't happy with me or with the fact that I was going to throw away my whole course because of "a little misunderstanding".

This wasn't going to put me off. I stuck to my plan. I think I even said to the carer that I would go into college, but when it was time for that teacher's lesson, he was to take me to Romford snooker hall. We could spend the rest of the day there. He didn't like that idea either.

On the day, we got into the college and followed the timetable. Lunchtime was before the interview. A few words were exchanged, quietly so no one would hear us, and we ended up in his car. The carer tried to convince me that it was best to go to class, take the interview, and be done with it. I just gave him a straight "I'm not taking that interview".

"So what are we going to do then?"

"Take me to the snooker hall."

"I've already said I'm not taking you to the snooker hall."

"OK, well, take me home then."

"Oh yeah, so your mother will start asking questions about why you're home early?"

"OK, not home. Take me to McDonald's. We can get a drink there and wait till college is over. Then take me home."

"I am not waiting in MacDonald's for two hours."

"OK, we can wait in the car for two hours, then."

"Oh, OK. Wait in the car for two hours? What if someone sees us not in class?"

"I don't care."

"Oh, you don't? What happens after the lesson? We go back inside?"

"If you're not taking me home, then I guess so."

"Oh, go back inside so we can get caught on the way to the next lesson."

"Yes, that is what we are doing if you are not taking me home or to McDonald's!"

"Well, we are sitting in the car, then, because there's no way I'm going to drive out of the college."

"Fine. Sitting in the car it is, then."

And so we did. We sat in the car for two, maybe three hours. The whole time we weren't even speaking to each other. There was no way I was going to take that stupid interview, and I was sticking to that plan.

After an hour, he broke the silence and asked me if I had changed my mind. I just gave a simple and emotionless no—an ice-cold answer.

When the two hours were up, we went back into the college because he wasn't driving me anywhere. So I attended my last lesson of the day. Going down the corridor, I prayed that we would not bump into the teacher whose lesson I had not attended. Luckily, we didn't.

My Closing Statements

Before I continue, I want to pause and say some words of wisdom. I'm speaking to the teachers and parents and carers here—basically, anyone who works with children, mostly children with disability, but I try to speak for all children.

Let's start off with teachers. I know that it's part of your job to share wisdom with the next generation. You're shadowed by the government telling you what to teach. It's your job to create knowledge for the next group of people who will take over and keep the country moving. If your hands are tied, and you're doing what is required of you, then I don't have a problem with it.

The only issue I have with how I was taught in school is this: I feel that I was isolated for the majority of my time at school. I had very little support nor instruction in how to communicate with others. I had very little opportunity to mix with my peers. You may say this is partially my fault, and I don't blame you for thinking that. I know that I had chances, but not enough to build up my confidence. At times I felt like I was completely alone in school with no one to look up to. No person should feel like they are alone in the world.

I also felt unprepared for what lies ahead for me. Fine, there was the work experience, which was fun, and I met some really great people. However, I didn't feel like it was truly work.

Another example happened in year twelve, when they told me to go a classroom with other disabled students to learn how to touch type and play guess the word (hangman). If we were not doing those things, we were supposed to do our coursework. I had caught up with my work, so there was no need for me to be in that class. From my point of view, it felt like you didn't know what to do with me, so you booked me in unnecessary places and gave me busywork. You wasted a chance for me to learn how to talk to people.

Why not teach disabled students about the laws that cover disabilities, like the Equality Act 2010, the Human Right Act 1998, and the Care Act 2014? Those would be more useful to me than learning how to touch type on a laptop.

One time in drama class, we were doing an exercise in which we had to pretend to be news reporters. When it was my turn to get on stage in front of the class, I had to say my lines from memory. I began, "My name is Thomas Ka-Ka-K." I couldn't say my name. The teacher encouraged me to finish my lines, and eventually I did. Then the class had to choose if I should go through to the next round. The class instantly said, "No, he stuttered his lines", and that was that.

I do not watch the news often, but I know that not everyone is perfect when speaking their lines. They mostly have a screen or a piece of paper in front of them with the lines on. I think we should be taught that it's OK to mess up as long as we can pick ourselves up afterwards. That's a better message to get across at an early age, I feel.

To parents, I want to say that if your child, disabled or not, shows an interest in sport, music, drawing, painting, acting, reading, writing, or anything else you can think of—especially if they show talent—try everything to encourage them. Tell them that they have to go through a few hard times to get to the good achievements. Put in the effort to give your child the best chance to thrive. Please encourage them to pursue their ideas or dreams.

Lastly, a similar talk to carers. Of course, it depends on the person you're caring for and the type of disability you're working with. However, if the person you're caring for has control of their actions and thoughts, then I give you the same advice I gave the parents. Help out the person and try not to interfere!

2012

Snooker with Steve Davis

Going every day to Romford Snooker, I had become friends with the owner, Richard. It was no surprise, really, given that I hung around the club five days a week for seven hours each day.

Only eight months after I start playing snooker, I noticed a poster on the board behind the counter. It showed a picture of Steve Davis, and the text said:

Six Times World Champion
Steve Davis
Coming Down on 12 March 2012

My carer on that day said that we should go to this event and watch Steve Davis play. We asked the owner to sign us up for tickets. I gave him the fee, and my carer put both of our names on the list. I got the snooker table I normally played on and started my daily practice. While I was practising, Richard came up to me and asked if I would like to play a game with Steve Davis. Of course, I said yes! There was no way that I was going to let this opportunity slip away! After that, I was practising with a purpose.

On the day, the carer and I made it to the club about 16.30. I practised two frames, and I counted that as my warm-up. My confidence was high.

The event was starting around six thirty. Everyone started to come in and take their seats around the table. I was getting more and more nervous as the time drew near. I still couldn't believe where I was: my first-ever match against a pro, and in front of two hundred people! The longer I had to wait, the more butterflies crept up on me.

Two other people had a frame with Steve Davis before me. As I watched the games, I said to myself, *Relax. It's only a friendly charity event. Pot as many as you can and try to have fun. Most likely this is a once-in-a-lifetime chance I've got here. Just have fun!*

After the second frame ended, I thought, *Here we go!*

"I would like to welcome a young man," Richard said. "He's a great supporter of our club. Would you please welcome Tom Kandiah!"

I wheeled up to the table and shook Steve's hand.

"Tom is going to be torch bearer for the Olympics, representing Barking and Dagenham. Isn't that right, Tom?"

I nervously said, "Yes."

Everyone clapped.

"Thank you very much," said Richard.

Steve let me call the flip of the coin. "Heads!"

I took a long time deciding who should break first. I chose Steve because, under pressure, I might mess up on the first shot. Steve said, "Tough decision, I know."

Near the beginning of the frame, he had me snookered behind the ball. Steve was a bit more relaxed than I was. He was trying to get me to up and down the table to pot the red ball. I was trying hard to play the game correctly, so I played a boring safety shot. Looking back on that day, I really wish that I had been more relaxed and taken the shot that Steve showed me. Everyone would have been more entertained.

As the game progressed, I loosened up a little and felt more relaxed. At the very end of the game, Steve had left the black ball on the cushion.

"Choice of safety shot or just go for it?"

"Go for it, Tom!" the people shouted out.

"Don't listen to them," Steve said.

But my mind was already made up, and I gave a massive hit on the cue ball.

Steve was walking around to the side pocket. He watched the cue ball hit four cushions and slowly drop into the middle pocket. I shook Steve Davis's hand, and the frame ended.

After that game, I watched Steve play three more people and give a trick-shot show.

And I had a photo with him and got it signed by the man himself.

That was the night pretty much done. Before we left, my carer and I had a chance to speak to Steve Davis again. We had had a good evening and felt a bit starstruck. We went next door to the pub to celebrate.

2012: The Olympic Torch

People were starting to talk about the 2012 Olympic Games happening in London. With the games, there are torch bearers. My father saw on the internet how to sign up for a chance to be one of the bearers. He filled in the form and sent it off. I had no expectation whatsoever. Those things didn't come to me; they just didn't happen.

Then I got an email saying, *"Congratulations, Thomas! You are a 2012 Olympic Torch Bearer!"* I couldn't believe what I was reading. I wanted to scream out on social media. However, the email said to wait. On 19 March 2012, I was free to scream out, "I AM A TORCH BEARER FOR THE 2012 OLYMPICS!"

I still remember every moment, from the butterflies leading up to my part of the run to the excitement of holding the torch for the very first time. Even the preparation beforehand—putting on the tracksuit for the first time and receiving the number tag 055—made me realise that this was actually happening!

I had a haircut the week before, and I wanted to do something special. So I had the 2012 Olympic logo shaved on the back of my head!

When it was my turn to shine, I had support from the people on the bus, and very slowly I recognised family and friends in the crowds. I was wheeled out of the bus and given my torch. I couldn't help but yell with joy, and I held it as high as I could. As the entertainment moved forward, I got congratulations and a pat on the back. Two girls gave me pecks on the cheek.

As you can see in the picture below, a blue coach followed me, playing loud music. Everyone was cheering.

This has got to be a favourite picture that I got on the day.

123

A man on a bike came over to me and explained what was going to happen. Honestly, it was difficult to hear him over all the music. He turned on the gas container inside the torch with a little pin key.

He told me that when the flame came by, I needed to be in the middle of the road. Someone would transfer the flame over, and someone would push me.

I was thinking, *Here comes my moment!*

There were five or six security guards alongside each person as they carried the flame. One of them transferred the flame over to my torch. After a little turn to pose for the photographs, off I went. I tried my best to hold it as high as possible. I heard people cheering and saw them taking pictures on their phones.

After a while, I held the torch with both hands, because it got heavy. Then a red speed bump came up, and all I could think was, *Whatever you do, do* not *drop the damn torch!*

Near to the end of my run, there was a build-up of people. I held the flame high, felt very proud, and gave out a massive, "WOOOO!" The crowd cheered. I transferred the flame over to next the person, feeling relieved and happy to have taken part.

That was my 4 minutes and 3 seconds of Olympic torch claim to fame. I will never forget that experience.

As I got back on the bus, I waved goodbye to family and friends. When I got home, they were all waiting for me. We had food and drink, and they all took photos and congratulated me.

11

Diary/Journal of 2013–2015

2013

The year 2012 had some of the best moments of my life, with my eighteenth birthday party, snooker with Steve Davis, and being a torch bearer. When 2013 came round, I wondered if I could do better.

The year started off on a positive note, because my friend Gavin rang me up for a snooker game at Romford Snooker Club. While we were playing, he asked if I would like to go to the Snooker Masters. I said yes. He had got three tickets for me, himself, and one of my carers. It would be my first live snooker event. I couldn't wait!

On that day, the three of us met up at my house and took a taxi to Alexandra Palace, which is in North London. When we got there, I couldn't believe it. I was so happy to finally make it to an actual sports event.

Alexandra Palace was such a beautiful place. There was a professional snooker table set up at the corner, with a line of people waiting to have a go. I got in the queue and waited my turn.

As I started to play, a small crowd built up. I thought, *Playing snooker in front of a crowd again! And this time it's only me playing.* I somehow found the courage to play well, and surprised myself. I knew that Gavin was filming me, so I had to play well! When I finished, everyone clapped. It was a proud moment. I bowed and gave a small wave.

We went to find our seats. The wheelchair space was at the end of a row. I soon realised that I was placed directly behind a cameraman. He was blocking my view of the table. I had no choice but to watch the game on one of the TV monitors above. I felt like I was watching the game at home. It was still a good experience, but I wish I could have actually seen the match.

Mum's Illness

One quiet afternoon, when Mother and my brother were out, I heard my father calling for me. He wanted to talk. So I paused the video game I was playing and entered the front room. My father turned down the volume of the TV and started talking.

I could not believe my ears. He wanted me to give my mother a certain amount of money each week. I asked him the reason for such a strange request. He answered, "For looking after you and your needs."

The first thought that came to my mind was care work. "So you want me to pay my own mother to look after her own son?"

He nodded.

I thought about it. "No, I won't do it!"

He had a look of shock on his face, as if he was surprised by my answer. "So you won't pay your own mother any money for your care, something she does for you every day?"

Honestly, I was starting to get frustrated. "I am not paying any money to Mum for just being a mother to her child!"

At this point, the whole situation exploded. The entire street probably heard us. We went back and forth, but it didn't come to a conclusion. I surprised myself by not backing down as I usually did. This was the first time I stuck to my guns where my father was concerned. I felt the rage in me to such an extent that it had to go somewhere and erupt.

While I still had control of my emotions, I took a deep breath, composed myself, and calmly said, "Before we finish with our 'talk', I would like to leave you something to think about." I then startled myself by shouting at the top of my voice, "IF ANYTHING HAPPENED TO YOU, HOW DO YOU THINK MUM WOULD LOOK AFTER HERSELF?"

My father was definitely taken aback by my explosion. Most likely he didn't know that I had it in me.

Still full of such anger, I thought of another point and just let it out before Father had any chance to say anything. "OR EVEN TAKE CARE OF YOUR CHILDREN, FOR THAT MATTER!"

After shouting all that, I calmed down and wondered what would happen now. Father walked away, and I went back my room. I still couldn't believe what had just happened.

A few days passed. Then my father came back and said, "Your mother has an advanced case of frontotemporal dementia, and this means she's not going to recover."

I had no idea what that meant.

Father Moving House and My Decision

My father came to my brother and I and said that he was planning to move house. Which naturally meant that my brother and I would go with him. However, for myself, I felt scared to leave my network of friends and carers. I didn't know how to live on my own, right down to the bare bones of vital skills. Living alone would be a scary experience. I most likely needed to move in with my father.

However, one day he suggested that there were two options. If I moved in with him, we could go halves on a more expensive house. Or I could buy my own house and try living on my own. When he put these options on the table for me, I was thrown back. This was really the first adult decision that he encouraged me to make.

During the following weeks, I puzzled over the more suitable way to take. My father said that he wouldn't buy any house until he knew my decision, which added pressure. My father set up a meeting with my uncle to help guide me through the possibilities.

It was good to talk to my uncle, as he had a lot of knowledge about this sort of thing. We spoke about Mother's illness and how it was only going to get worse. If I lived with my parents, it would be challenging for me. On the other hand, if I lived alone, I might feel scared and lonely.

This was the biggest decision of my life so far, and it had to be the right one. My uncle said that I would be helped every step of the way by himself and Father.

For me, the possibility of feeling lonely was better than living with my parents while there was a good chance of Mother's mental illness getting worse. With that said, I still needed some time to myself to think about this life-changing decision.

By the time September came, it was clear that Mother's condition was deteriorating. Her driving was pretty erratic, and I felt scared when I was in the car with her. One day she drove from the house in London down the M25 to Essex and back, by herself, for no reason. I only knew about this because Father came to me saying that the mileage was getting too high on the car and I had to pay for it. I was confused by that statement, and I disagreed. Most of the time I wasn't in the car when Mother was driving. I had another fight with Father. To settle matters, we agreed to pay half each. To be honest, I still thought that was unfair.

After a few such episodes with Mother, I made my mind up to leave the nest and try to live alone, however scary that felt.

New House

After I made the decision to move out of London and live alone, we started to view properties. I looked at a few before I found a lovely bungalow in Tendring Essex. It was detached and had wide hallways. I knew immediately that this was where I wanted to live. I put in an offer, and on 24 September, I received the news that it was accepted. I was so happy! There was still a lot of work that needed to be done, but I was excited that I had got my very own house now.

My parents started to look around that area for their house, as they wanted to be nearby. After a few weeks they were lucky enough to find a lovely four-bedroom house about five minutes' drive away from me.

Some months later, we all moved into my parents' new house. "My" room was downstairs in the front room. I would often have disagreements with my brother because he was watching tv and I was playing a game. My brother wanted me to wear headphones. I thought this was unjust, because my brother had another TV in his room upstairs, while I was stuck downstairs with nowhere else to go.

Moving house had an effect on Mother. Her condition was best served by the same routine, and the move seemed to trigger more confusion. For example, she would leave the house in the middle of the night and wander randomly, so we had to make sure the door was always locked. As another example, she would hide her bottle of wine, refill it with water, and hide it again.

Mother's Condition

Living at my parents' house full-time was difficult. The atmosphere was strained because of Mother's behaviour. Mother wanted me to sleep upstairs and couldn't understand why I could not get up the stairs. She tried to stay downstairs herself. It got to the stage where we had to ask other family members for support. Finally, someone jumped in and helped me out with the situation. They somehow managed to talk Mother into going upstairs to sleep.

In the mornings I would be sleeping soundly, and a family member would rush into the room, turn on the light, and shout, "Wakey-wakey, sleepyhead!" The light blinded me, and it took me a while to wake. Before I knew it, they were already getting breakfast, which I refused because I had only got up two minutes before. I could do nothing but hold my feelings in check and cope with the situation as it came. This would carry on throughout 2014.

As you can imagine, with all this going on, I could not wait to move out to my new house and start a new chapter in my life.

2015: Slowly Moving In

By the time 2015 came round, my house was taking shape. On 1 February, I went out with Father to start buying the basics for living in a home. When the kitchen and the toilet were finished, I spent a couple of hours there to get some idea of what it would be like to stay in the building with a carer and a dog. I took my PlayStation 4 with me, plugging it into a temporary TV set-up, and borrowed my nan's old sofa. This continued for a few weeks for a few hours at a time.

When Father thought it was time, I had my bed made up for me and spent the first night at my new home alone. It was really weird because I had never spent a night in any house completely on my own. So I was having mixed feelings about the whole experience.

Beginning 20 February, I spent two nights entirely on my own. My first thought was to see if all the doors and windows were locked. There was not much else to check, honestly. Then I climbed into my new bed on the first night at my new house. At this stage I had no curtains or blinds put up to cover the windows. I can tell you that was the creepiest night that I had ever slept through.

I was lying there when a noise came out of nowhere. I was scared to open my eyes; I thought someone was looking in the window. I didn't have much sleep, especially because when day broke, the sunlight woke me up. I really needed to get blinds. Meantime, for the first few weeks, I had no choice but to get up bright and early.

After a while, I was able to get through the whole day and night with my dog at my side. I had to open the back door to let him out. One night I got into bed, forgetting to close the door, I woke up freezing and realised what I had done. This really scared me. Now I'm paranoid. I go round checking every night that everything is locked.

For my twenty-first birthday, I had bought a PS4 game machine. That was my big celebration—a PS4 and a boring family meal at the local curry restaurant. The food was excellent. I always liked eating there. However, eating with family was less fun. Why? Because I was around them most of the time, so going out for a meal with them felt less special. That was not counting the fact that I was often shoved aside at the end of the table. People talked among themselves, and when they did engage me in conversation, it was usually with a dumb question rather than speaking to me like I was a human being.

My extension was finished close to 10 March. I was having trouble figuring out what the best use was for all the space that I now had. I had two options at the time: a snooker table or a gym set-up. The idea behind the snooker table was that I could put more hours into my game. Since I had moved to a new area, away from my familiar club, the luxury of going to a snooker club was getting slimmer as the weeks went by. The idea behind the gym setup was to develop a disability-friendly environment which I could use with the least help possible.

The next day, I was in my garage. The dog followed me in and automatically sat on the footplate of my scooter. That was usually where he would go if I were taking him out for a walk. He would sit like a picture until I reached the grass. Then I would let him free to chase a ball. He would jump back on or walk home with me after. I thought the whole thing was funny, how the dog just assumed I was taking him out. You could see it in his face: "Take me out, man! Is it time for my walk and chasing after a tennis ball?"

Staying in the house was getting more comfortable with every month. I still had carers, and family came round pretty much every day, so it didn't feel like living on my own. Perhaps it felt more like a holiday home.

Trying to Encourage Father to Teach Me Something

On 28 March, I was getting tired of doing nothing. When the opportunity to upgrade my computer came up, I jumped in for the challenge. However, I needed Father's help. He came up with the idea of building a new one from scratch. While I was excited about this new upgrade, I was a bit worried that my father wasn't going to teach me how to do each part. I felt that at the age of 21, I still didn't know how to do basic DIY. I always had to cry to my parents to help me with tasks that I should have learned by now as a young adult.

I tried to focus Father on teaching me the necessary skills. I said all this to him, and he seemed to understand.

When the time came a week later, we had all the kit bought and ready to build. As we began, it was clear that Father didn't quite get the purpose of the task, which was to teach me to do it myself. I only did the beginning screws and maybe the RAM cards, which must be the easiest parts of the computer. Everything else my father did, with the aid of my brother. I ended up just sitting there, passing tools to my father or brother. My father taught my brother how to build a PC—not me.

I was slightly disappointed. However, I ended up with a new PC. So that was something positive for a change.

Decision to Get a Snooker Table

It took me until 19 April to finally settle on the choice of getting a snooker table for the extension. Father didn't like it. His idea was to put a dining table there for when people came around for dinner. That didn't feel right to me, because I knew in my heart that the possibility of someone else coming down for dinner was slim. (And I was right! As of the date that I'm writing this, 16 March 2017, not one person has come around for dinner.)

So I stuck to my gut and the idea of a snooker table. Father tried to change my mind for a few weeks, but he finally gave up and accepted the idea.

I searched for the right table. On 19 August, I got the right table. A workman came to my house to fit the table. As soon as he finished, you bet I jumped straight into practice mode. Due to my extension, I could just fit in a 10 foot by 5 foot table, which was the next size down from a professional table (12 foot by 6 foot).

After only a few days of having my own table at home, I managed to score a break of 59 in the line-up practice. I had no idea where that one came from. The numbers kept on going higher, and the snooker balls kept on disappearing. The break ended with the pressure getting too high, and I made a dumb mistake.

The Passion for Snooker Is Fading

It only took about a month of using my table at home before I was questioning my game. I was starting to doubt myself and my ability. However, I couldn't place the reasons for this. *I don't know what to do. I've been playing snooker for five years now, and I'm still a rookie, getting breaks of 16 to 25. I've been stuck on that for three years now. I should be a 30 to 60-break player by now! And I'm still making silly novice mistakes.*

This went on for months. I dragged myself to my table, trying my best to overcome my lack of good breaks. Once every two weeks, I would get a respectful break to my liking, which always gave me hope that one day I would be able to overcome my decline. When you are on this path, it is natural to have doubts creep into your head. I'm no different. I questioned my work ethic, wondering if I had it in me to overcome the problem.

This carried on through November. It added pressure on me to get my game back on track. I had just entered for my second time going to the wheelchair snooker tournament at the end of the month. I was worried about it because my technique wasn't quite right. I had a coach over to help me, but even he wasn't sure what was happening. I also had to practise while wearing the full monkey suit.

When we moved house, it became difficult for me to see my snooker coach. Father said it was too far to travel; Mother's illness was getting progressively worse, and she could not be left.

The carer took over being my coach. He picked up on every little mistake. It got to the point where I was more concerned about what I might have to explain rather than the joy that I had for the game. With the competition only weeks away, you can imagine how this magnified the tension that I had with that carer. It was a real test of my passion for the game.

My passion was on a very short fuse. By 15 November, I had had enough with everything related to the game of snooker—all the arguing with the carer about how the game should be played, about him always being the judge of what decisions I had to make, everything!

So I went to the one place where I wasn't afraid to say what I felt, which was Facebook, and I made it public that I was "retiring" from the sport of snooker. It was a bit funny. I was retiring even though my career had never really kicked off. But that was how seriously I took my snooker.

I left this post on my Facebook page for everyone to see:

> *hi people, I'm thinking for some time now (i know shocker I'm thinking) anyway after my competition which is at the end of the month, I am only going to play for fun. now, what does that mean, it means that I am not gonna learn any more about the 'art of snooker' ...*
>
> *... Anyone who knows me should know that I hate quitting or giving up on something you love doing because you are not gonna go anywhere in life if you just quit as things get tough. However, with me it has come to every day, I will go to the snooker table, and within 5 mins of me trying to get back into, it, I will get so annoyed because my game is not as it was. ...*
>
> *so I going to see if my behaviour gets a bit more positive if I take my focus somewhere. So apologies if I've been a bit grumpy of late, hopefully, you understand now why.*
>
> *just wanna say thanks to everyone that supported me in the game and trying to keep my hopes and dreams up.*

On top of what I said above, I want to say a huge thank-you to my snooker coach, Andrew Green. Without your guidance, I wouldn't have been able to reach 59 in practice!

Even though I had lost all faith in the game of snooker, and friction was slowly building up with the carer who was helping me, I still went to the competition.

The set-up up was pretty much the same as the first time. On 27 November, with the carer and my parents on board, we drove to the South-West Snooker Academy, Gloucester. After more than five hours in the car, stopping halfway for a food and toilet break, we finally reached the hotel. My parents stayed a while and then headed back. They had intended to stay, but because Mother's condition was worsening, Father decided it was best not to.

The Walk to the Snooker Building

As my parents drove off home, my carer and I gathered our equipment and walked to the other side of the road. We had to walk down a side road to the academy.

I reminded the carer that the last time we were here, we had walked on the road because it was a slightly less bumpy ride. This time, he was pushing me on the pavement, which I did not like in the slightest. The main problem for the chair was that the slopes to the road were at an angle which was too harsh for my liking. There were about five of these pavements, none suitable for a wheelchair of any kind.

Despite my reservations, for the first two pavements the carer insisted on sticking to his route. Big surprise, it was awkward to safely move the chair up and down those angles. What made it worse for me was that I held my snooker cue, which was very expensive. It was a John Parris traditional cue, one piece, 59 inches long, in a double black leather case. I had to carry the case resting on my feet and reaching over my shoulder. Trust me, it was heavy, especially on my left shoulder.

As the carer pushed me on those uneven cobbled pavements, I felt very uneasy and nervous. I imagined myself falling out of the chair or dropping my cue. After two pavements, I told the carer to stay on the road. We finished the rest of the journey on the side road, which was much better. It had a few bumps but was far less dangerous than those pavement death traps.

We made it to the building and went in, up the dodgy, slow elevator that I had missed so much.

Practising

Once up, I went through the doors to the meeting room. I saw people whom I recognised from last time. All I wanted to do was practise. I wanted to get going.

The carer set up the table. The very first thing I noticed was how huge it was. As I mentioned, my table at home was noticeably smaller. I had to change everything from my positioning to the power I had to use. I had to scale everything about my game.

I only slightly improved with practice. It was hard for me to focus, as the space was hectic. People were pushing past me all the time. The atmosphere was chaos!

Photographer

Amid this chaos, I was frustrated with a simple mistake I kept on making. Still, I found it funny when a woman came over with her camera and asked if she could take an action shot. I couldn't refuse.

We were on opposite sides of the table. I got ready to take a shot. She said, "On three, take the shot."

Cue positioned, I listened to her counting down.

"One."

Please don't miss this shot!

"Two."

Whatever you do, don't mess up!

"Three!"

I took the shot—and I was so happy to see it drop into the pocket!

I laughed because all the pressure was off. Jokingly, I asked her to stand in front during the competition; then I wouldn't miss a shot. I carried on practising, and the photographer went off to take more photos of people in action.

After practising for a few hours, we packed up and went back to the hotel. That evening we went to the pub next door and had dinner. Then we got ready for an early start tomorrow for *competition day*!

Day Two, Morning

We had set our alarms to 07:30 the next day for a nine o'clock start. With little time to waste, we got ready. When I had to brush my teeth, I quickly found out that my wheelchair would not fit through the doorway to the bathroom. So I had to brush my teeth just outside the bathroom, with my carer helping me put on the toothpaste and giving me a towel to wipe my mouth with afterwards. My teeth done, I needed some sort of a wash.

Since the shower was not suitable for my needs, I had a plan B. That was to use a small towel and do my best to wash the essentials. I told my carer this, and at first he didn't seem to understand what I meant. I had to talk him through the steps:

1. Use a big towel to cover the chair.
2. Fill up the sink with warm water.
3. Put some soap into the water.

He gave me a questioning look like I was mad, but I carried on.

4. Put the whole small towel into the soapy water for ten seconds.
5. Hand me the towel so I can wash the essentials.
6. The carer could wash the hard-to-reach places, i.e., back, feet, and left arm.
7. Dry me off with another big towel.

Once washed, I put on the snooker clothes. I had a sponsor T-shirt which I had to wear. It was much better than wearing a shirt and tie. We grabbed all the gear and started walking down to the academy.

I must admit that I hoped my carer would remember how unforgiving the pavements had been yesterday. I couldn't have been more wrong. After crossing the busy main road, the carer again pushed me on the first of many pavements. As I had last time, I became nervous. I leaned back and way over to the left or right, just to gain balance. After the second pavement, I had had enough. "Look, can you get me off the pavements? This is dangerous. I don't feel safe."

But he carried on. The next pavement really annoyed me because the angle to go down on the road was the worst one of all. I tried to prepare myself, but I almost lost my balance. I started to feel that I had to choose between me or my cue to hold on to. Luckily, I gained control of my body and caught the case by the handle. It hit my right shoulder hard.

After the third pavement, I was entirely frustrated with how the day had started, and this was only the beginning! We finally made it to the academy and went through the doors to meet everyone.

My Snooker Matches

Once everyone knew where to go, we headed for our tables. My carer tried to give me a talk before the match, which was kind enough. However, after what had happened already, I just wanted to mentally calm myself on my own.

When we got to the table, the carer helped me onto my seat and got my snooker cue. I shook hands with the referee, and the match started. It didn't start well. My carer kept trying to interfere and give me tips throughout the game, which made things worse. The match ended 2:1. I was very disappointed as I knew I could play better.

After the game, we paid our respects and sat in the meeting area, watching the professionals play on TV.

Two hours later, it was time for my second match, which was the last match of the day. As the game progressed, it was clear that it was unbalanced, and I was going to win. I relaxed and had fun. This upset the carer, and he signalled me to pay more attention. I took no notice of him, and the score ended up 2:0, so I should have been happy with this. However, it didn't feel like a win.

We'd started the day at 07.30, and by the time I finished both of my games, it was 18:30! That was a long day. When I told the person who was keeping the scores that I won the last game, and signed the paper with the referee, my day was officially over. I wanted to go back to the hotel to change into my everyday clothes. I completely forgot that we had to walk back to the hotel. I didn't want to do that, so we asked around to see if someone was willing to drive me. I wasn't that lucky; we had no choice but to walk. When we went through the doors, I was surprised at how dark it was. I could only see a few feet away.

Then came the dread of the carer pushing me up and down the pavements. The carer pushed me onto the first two, then started pushing me on the road. There were three cars that he had to move me to the side for. We could always tell by the light coming from the vehicle. The other benefit of the car's light was that I briefly had a better view of the road ahead of me and could prepare for any bumps. Perhaps because it was late and I used my energy up, I couldn't be bothered to say anything to the carer about them.

Last Day of the Competition

Our final day of competition was 29 November. I packed my case along with my cue and headed to the academy. My equipment and I made it in one piece.

I quickly find out that I had one more game to play. That was good, as my father was making the three-hour journey to collect us. We headed to the table. The carer was still giving me tips and advice. This was really irritating, as he was saying the same thing over and over.

How did it go? I think I played the worst snooker yet in this competition!

As you might expect, this didn't go down well with the carer. After the game, he made that point very clear to me. He said, "If I had known you were just going to give up, I wouldn't have bothered coming down here with you!"

In short, there was a negative vibe between me and the carer. For the most part, I just let him go on until he walked off, I think to the toilets. Then I felt so badly about how I had played that I went up to Craig, my opponent, and apologised to him. He told me, "Not to worry. I wasn't playing my best either. These things happen." Which made it a bit better, but I still felt terrible.

On the way home, we updated Father about the competition. I felt drained and tried to sleep. It didn't last long because I could feel Mother watching me and hear her whispering to Father that we (the carer and I) were both sleeping. I can't rest with someone watching me. Nowadays we knew why Mother acted so strangely at times, but it was still hard to get my head around the situation.

We dropped off the carer and finally made it home.

What happened after the competition was a series of events that led me to lose interest in the game of snooker altogether. I know that because before the tournament, I'd said that I was finished, but this was really my last attempt to see if I still had any passion for the game. I must point out that I continued having arguments with the same carer. It was a true test for me, because I had awful social skills when it came to appropriately dealing with disagreements.

In short, I was having trouble keeping my passion for this wonderful game alive. I felt I should be a much better player then what my results were telling me. I wasn't shy about making my opinions public. Throughout December, some people tried their best to encourage me not to give up, to keep playing, and one day my game would be even better than it had been before.

The game was taking over my mind, and it was all I could think of.

I am grateful that I had friends who were very supportive and tried their best to help me out. I lost sleep because I was putting myself under so much pressure. My carer was still criticising me, which didn't help.

By the end of the year, I had had enough. So I put the table cover on, a kind of symbolism, I suppose. I felt like I would never get the passion burning within me again.

2016–2017

There's not much to talk about for 2016—three things that I can think of.

One occurred in the first half of the year. I had to change my carers to fit my ever-changing lifestyle. That's the thing about carers that I have found: as your life changes, which it will, your needs will likewise change, and therefore the carer system has to change slightly.

I still have carers for the majority of the week, and my father pops in now and again, so I'm never without some form of care. Sometimes I get tired and grumpy. What's great about the system I have now is on those not-so-great days, they will give me the support I need and allow me to go through the emotions without challenging them. After a little show of emotions, I bring myself back and the day returns to normal. Something must be working, because some of the carers I've got have been with me for almost one year now. They must be crazy!

Mother Situation

My mother's illness was progressing so fast that the family was struggling to cope. A meeting was called, and it was decided that the only option was to place her in an appropriate care home. So that's where Mother is now. Father goes to see her and on occasion takes other family members. He has asked me if I would like to go, but I always say no thanks.

It's no secret that Mother's behaviour changed dramatically over the years. When I last saw her, it was like talking to a stranger. I could tell that she had no memories. The best way I can describe her is that she was like an empty vessel. I have asked family members not to give me any news or talk about her condition, because it makes me uncomfortable. To be honest, I don't know how to deal with it in my head. I'm trying my best to look forward and see what the future holds for me, not look back and hold the memories of what my mother used to be like.

As you can imagine, this didn't settle well with Father at first. In fact it was the beginning of a very rocky relationship between father and son. After months of seeing my father as a strong character, I was beginning to question that. Perhaps that was because I was finally growing up and developing my own mind.

I found myself in unfamiliar territory. It's no surprise that my relationship with family is strange at best. My perception of them changed with every meeting. It was hard to believe that I once saw them as role models.

Doctors

On Friday, 13 May 2016, my brother, father, and I went to Addenbrooke's, a clinical research centre. The purpose of the trip was so my brother and I could speak to the doctors and get a professional explanation of Mother's illness. As I said before, all I knew initially was that it was called frontotemporal dementia, but I had only a basic idea of what that meant. On the journey, Father asked if we had made our minds up about knowing the pros and cons of the illness. I had already made my mind up, but I was not sure about my brother.

The doctors called us in. I felt nervous and apprehensive. The neurosurgeon described his work and the possibilities the future held for us. He told us that the offspring of a frontotemporal dementia patient had a one in two chance of being carriers themselves. Carriers "have a high risk of developing frontotemporal dementia in the future" (a quote from a letter I received afterwards).

He asked if we had any questions. We both said no. Looking back, I wish I'd asked more questions. For example, would this be passed on to any future children that my brother or I might have?

Then the second doctor spoke. He gradually led up to the big question: "Do you want to know if you are a carrier?" I reluctantly said no. I did have doubts, but I really did not want to worry about this for the rest of my life. If I've got it, it is not curable anyway. As for my brother, I can't speak for him.

Meeting done, we had to go back on 5 June for blood tests and a mental assessment.

In the weeks that followed, everything seemed to be normal. I appeared to be in a good mood and followed my timetable of carers. One day, though, I was feeling a bit down. When my carer, Kim, came into the house, it didn't take long for me to spill out my emotions. I must have gone on for an hour talking about school and how I was bullied.

Kim said, "You should write a book about all this. You clearly remember a lot."

With that one sentence, I had somehow found inspiration to attempt to write a book. I had no idea what I was doing, but I attempted to plan it anyway. I don't know why, but I wanted to start on an easy date that I could remember. So on 1 June, I began to write.

I owe Kim, who gave me the necessary push to try something different—like writing.

When I decided to write this book, I chose to keep it to myself and my carers. The reason behind this was because I knew that my family wouldn't be supportive.

When I started writing, I thought it would be funny if I grew out my hair and beard until I finished my book (or at least the first draft). It was a little game with myself. What I didn't expect was for my family to freak out over the growth of my beard. Speculation ran wild, and rumours spread that I was depressed—just because I was growing a beard. My father even booked me in to see a local counsellor.

Meanwhile, I was beginning to write about the start of my break-up. That really made me emotionally stuck. I didn't write a word for two weeks. It was frustrating because I had been writing every day since I started.

That week, I saw the counsellor—not because I was depressed, but because I was curious to see if this person could help me. I was super nervous, mainly because this was the first time I had spoken to a counsellor on my own. I went to the office, and a lady introduced herself as Rachel King. Briefly, I explained that the reason for me being there was because my family thought I was depressed, which I wasn't.

In the second week, I told her why they might think I was depressed. What was unknown to them was that I was stuck in my book idea and needed help to get through it.

In the third week, Rachel managed to get me to open up, and that evening I was able to continue writing.

I completed the high school section two months and two weeks after that day. Again, I have to say a huge thank-you to Rachel King. I couldn't have done it without your help.

To finish up, I want to talk about what lies ahead for me. I would like to think that's the question on many people's minds, particularly young adults. Who am I? What am I supposed to do with my life? And for me, who is Thomas G. Kandiah?

I guess it starts off with my physical and mental health. It shouldn't be a surprise that being in a wheelchair for the majority of the time has an impact on the body. I have been in some sort of physical pain for all of my life. I've grown used to the pain. I know that might sound sad, but I have to accept it. For me, that's the reality of a lifetime in a wheelchair.

There is also my mental health. I worry about it. I'm stuck indoors most of the time and live in a limited social environment. I fear creating an illness within me, yet I can't do anything to prevent it. At this time, that's the thing that scares me the most.

"Surely family can help?" I hear you asking. Believe me, I have tried on multiple occasions to explain that I feel lost and need guidance into the next chapter of my life. What I quickly learned is that when you ask others for help, you have to be careful who you're asking. My family can't see the struggles that I face on a daily basis. I used to see my family, especially my father, as role models, but that has changed dramatically over the last year or so.

I realise that I have lots of challenges ahead, but I refuse to give up or take the easy route. I'm going to keep looking for opportunities.

Like many people with disabilities, I'm searching for independence. There will be obstacles in my way, but with the right mindset, there is always a way around them. I just have to find the right people to make it happen, and most importantly, find my identity.

Let's end on a positive note. I'm determined to make a fresh start, with a supportive group of people around me, keeping me on track. I have been working with my physio and trainer. At the start of 2018, I have a goal of walking. I have already improved at such a rate that I wouldn't be surprised if you see me walking everywhere soon.

They are also coming up with challenges to help me overcome my boundaries and improve my confidence. My mind is now focused on looking forward and always looking at different events.

If you want to continue reading about my adventures, I'm going to share my experiences on my blog:

www.thomasgkandiah.com

My goal is to show that against all the odds, we can still achieve our dreams despite our disabilities. We can change impossible to possible.

Thanks for making it this far. I am going to leave you with a poem that I wrote.

I'm standing, and there's nothing around me
I'm standing, and there's nothing around me,
Not a soul in sight,
And yet,
I'm still waiting,
Waiting for someone to hold my hand,
To show me the way,
And with every passing day,
My hopes are fading,
My vision more blurred,
My dreams out of reach,
And I'm back where I started,

I'm standing, and there's nothing around me,
And yet,
There's something keeping me going,
Wandering around an endless journey,
Not really knowing which direction to go for,
Hoping,
Praying,
Asking,
Is the path leading to a destination?

I'm standing, and there's nothing around me,
Like a chick unable to fly
Trapped in the nest.

END

BLOG

My life was full of possibilities
Started to show promise of activating great things.
With a partner who completed me,
Wanted me to improve myself.
Able to think outside of the box and take on new opportunities.
Started to feel my place in this world.
However.
I started to have a shiver down my spine.
Something didn't feel right.
My path started to disappear in front of my eyes,
Clouding my mind,
Making my opportunities unclear.
My life was changing at a rapid pace,
Beyond my control,
And I just allowed it.
And I'm paying for my choices.
My life being controlled by others.
Leading my life outside of my hands.

ACKNOWLEDGEMENTS

Thank you to Kim, Rachel, Charlotte, Alice, Gavin, Keith, and Peter, who all helped me along this journey. This wouldn't have been possible without your support! Thank you so much.

Printed in Great Britain
by Amazon